What People Are Saying about *Threshold Bible Study*

"Besides furnishing the reader with solid biblical analysis, this remarkable series provides a method of study and reflection, for both individuals and groups, that is bound to produce rich fruit. This well-developed thematic approach to Bible study is meant to wed serious study and personal prayer within a reflective context. Stephen Binz is to be applauded for this fine addition to Bible study programs."

DIANNE BERGANT, CSA, *Professor of Old Testament, Catholic Theological Union, Chicago*

"With lucidity and creativity, Stephen Binz offers today's believing communities a rich and accessible treasury of biblical scholarship. The series' brilliance lies in its simplicity of presentation complemented by critical depth of thought and reflective insight."

CAROL J. DEMPSEY, OP, *Professor of Theology, University of Portland, OR*

"God's holy word addresses the deepest levels of our lives with the assurance of divine grace and wisdom for our individual and communal faith. I am grateful for this new series introducing our Catholic people to the riches of sacred Scripture. May these guides to understanding the great truths of our redemption bring us all closer to the Lord of our salvation."

TIMOTHY CARDINAL DOLAN, *Archbishop of New York*

"In an increasingly Bible-reading and Bible-praying church these helpful books combine solid biblical information and challenging suggestions for personal and group prayer. By covering a wide variety of themes and topics they continually breathe new life into ancient texts."

JOHN R. DONAHUE, SJ, *Raymond E. Brown Professor Emeritus of New Testament Studies, St. Mary's Seminary and University, Baltimore, MD*

"To know and love Jesus and to follow him, we need to know and love the sacred Scriptures. For many years now, the *Threshold Bible Study* has proven to be a vital tool for Catholics seeking to go deeper in their encounter with Christ."

ARCHBISHOP JOSE H. GOMEZ, *Archbishop of Los Angeles*

"The church has called Scripture a 'font' and 'wellspring' for the spiritual life. *Threshold Bible Study* is one of the best sources for tapping into the biblical font. Pope John Paul II has stressed that 'listening to the word of God should become a life-giving encounter.' This is precisely what *Threshold Bible Study* offers to you—an encounter with the word that will make your heart come alive."

■ **TIM GRAY**, *President of the Augustine Institute, Denver*

"*Threshold Bible Study* offers solid scholarship and spiritual depth. Drawing on the church's living Tradition and the Jewish roots of the New Testament, *Threshold Bible Study* can be counted on for lively individual study and prayer, even while it offers spiritual riches to deepen communal conversation and reflection among the people of God."

■ **SCOTT HAHN**, *Founder of the St. Paul Center for Biblical Theology*

"Stephen Binz provides the church with a tremendous gift and resource in the *Threshold Bible Study*. This great series invites readers into the world of Scripture with insight, wisdom, and accessibility. This series will help you fall in love with the word of God!"

■ **DANIEL P. HORAN, OFM**, *Catholic Theological Union, Chicago*

"Stephen Binz has an amazing gift for making the meaning of the biblical text come alive! With a strong background in Bible study, he knows how to provide the road map any group can use to explore Scripture. Using the method known as *lectio divina*, *Threshold Bible Study* provides two things: growth in understanding the sacred text, and at the same time, the opportunity for actual conversion as the text is broken open and shared."

■ **BILL HUEBSCH**, *author and theologian*

"*Threshold Bible Study* is by far the best series of short Bible-study books available today. I recommend them to all the leaders I help train in the Catholic Bible Institutes of several dioceses. Kudos to Stephen Binz for writing books that are ideal for small-group or individual use."

■ **FELIX JUST, SJ**, *Biblical scholar and educator, Loyola House Jesuit Community, San Francisco*

"I am impressed by the way *Threshold Bible Study* opens the doors of the sacred page in an intelligent, engaging way that fosters a deeper, more meditative interaction with the word of God. Stephen Binz has carefully crafted this series for either one's daily meditation or a weekly group study with equally positive benefit. I am happy to endorse this series as a means to grow in one's friendship with Christ through the prayerful study of sacred Scripture."

■ **ARCHBISHOP JOSEPH F. NAUMANN**, *Archbishop of Kansas City in Kansas*

THRESHOLD
BIBLE STUDY

CHURCH *of the* HOLY SPIRIT

PART ONE

Acts of the Apostles
[1-14]

STEPHEN J. BINZ

TWENTY-THIRD
PUBLICATIONS
twentythirdpublications.com

Third printing 2019

TWENTY-THIRD PUBLICATIONS
One Montauk Avenue, Suite 200
New London, CT 06320
(860) 437-3012 or (800) 321-0411
www.twentythirdpublications.com

ISBN: 978-1-58595-914-3
Library of Congress Control Number: 2013931009
Printed in the U.S.A.

 A division of Bayard, Inc.

Contents

How to Use
Threshold Bible Study

T hreshold Bible Study is a dynamic, informative, inspiring, and life-changing series that helps you learn about Scripture in a whole new way. Each book will help you explore new dimensions of faith and discover deeper insights for your life as a disciple of Jesus.

The threshold is a place of transition. The threshold of God's word invites you to enter that place where God's truth, goodness, and beauty can shine into your life and fill your mind and heart. Through the Holy Spirit, the threshold becomes holy ground, sacred space, and graced time. God can teach you best at the threshold, because God opens your life to his word and fills you with the Spirit of truth.

With Threshold Bible Study each topic or book of the Bible is approached in a thematic way. You will understand and reflect on the biblical texts through overarching themes derived from biblical theology. Through this method, the study of Scripture will impact your life in a unique way and transform you from within.

These books are designed for maximum flexibility. Each study is presented in a workbook format, with sections for reading, reflecting, writing, discussing, and praying. Each Threshold book contains thirty lessons, which you can use for your daily study over the course of a month or which can be divided into six lessons per week, providing a group study of six weekly sessions (the first session deals with the Introduction). These studies are ideal for Bible study groups, small Christian communities, adult faith formation, student groups, Sunday school, neighborhood groups, and family reading, as well as for individual learning.

The commentary that follows each biblical passage launches your reflection on that passage and helps you begin to see its significance within the context of your contemporary experience. The questions following the commentary challenge you to understand the passage more fully and apply it to your own life. Space for writing after each question is ideal for personal study and also allows group participants to prepare for the weekly discussion. The prayer helps conclude your study each day by integrating your learning into your relationship with God.

The method of Threshold Bible Study is rooted in the ancient tradition of *lectio divina*, whereby studying the Bible becomes a means of deeper intimacy with God and a transformed life. Reading and interpreting the text (*lectio*) is followed by reflective meditation on its message (*meditatio*). This reading and reflecting flows into prayer from the heart (*oratio* and *contemplatio*). In this way, one listens to God through the Scripture and then responds to God in prayer.

This ancient method assures you that Bible study is a matter of both the mind and the heart. It is not just an intellectual exercise to learn more and be able to discuss the Bible with others. It is, more importantly, a transforming experience. Reflecting on God's word, guided by the Holy Spirit, illumines the mind with wisdom and stirs the heart with zeal.

Following the personal Bible study, Threshold Bible Study offers ways to extend personal *lectio divina* into a weekly conversation with others. This communal experience will allow participants to enhance their appreciation of the message and build up a spiritual community (*collatio*). The end result will be to increase not only individual faith but also faithful witness in the context of daily life (*operatio*).

When bringing Threshold Bible Study to a church community, try to make every effort to include as many people as possible. Many will want to study on their own; others will want to study with family, a group of friends, or a few work associates; some may want to commit themselves to share insights through a weekly conference call, daily text messaging, or an online social network; and others will want to gather weekly in established small groups.

By encouraging Threshold Bible Study and respecting the many ways people desire to make Bible study a regular part of their lives, you will widen the number of people in your church community who study the Bible regularly in whatever way they are able in their busy lives. Simply sign up people at the Sunday services and order bulk quantities for your church. Encourage people to follow the daily study as faithfully as they can. This encouragement can be through Sunday announcements, notices in parish publications, support on the church website, and other creative invitations and motivations.

Through the spiritual disciplines of Scripture reading, study, reflection, conversation, and prayer, Threshold Bible Study will help you experience God's grace more abundantly and root your life more deeply in Christ. The risen Jesus said: "Listen! I am standing at the door, knocking; if you hear my voice and open the door, I will come in to you and eat with you, and you with me" (Rev 3:20). Listen to the Word of God, open the door, and cross the threshold to an unimaginable dwelling with God!

SUGGESTIONS FOR INDIVIDUAL STUDY

• Make your Bible reading a time of prayer. Ask for God's guidance as you read the Scriptures.

• Try to study daily, or as often as possible according to the circumstances of your life.

• Read the Bible passage carefully, trying to understand both its meaning and its personal application as you read. Some persons find it helpful to read the passage aloud.

• Read the passage in another Bible translation. Each version adds to your understanding of the original text.

• Allow the commentary to help you comprehend and apply the scriptural text. The commentary is only a beginning, not the last word, on the meaning of the passage.

• After reflecting on each question, write out your responses. The very act of writing will help you clarify your thoughts, bring new insights, and amplify your understanding.

• As you reflect on your answers, think about how you can live God's word in the context of your daily life.

• Conclude each daily lesson by reading the prayer and continuing with your own prayer from the heart.

• Make sure your reflections and prayers are matters of both the mind and the heart. A true encounter with God's word is always a transforming experience.

• Choose a word or a phrase from the lesson to carry with you throughout the day as a reminder of your encounter with God's life-changing word.

• For additional insights and affirmation, share your learning experience with at least one other person whom you trust. The ideal way to share learning is in a small group that meets regularly.

SUGGESTIONS FOR GROUP STUDY

• Meet regularly; weekly is ideal. Try to be on time, and make attendance a high priority for the sake of the group. The average group meets for about an hour.

• Open each session with a prepared prayer, a song, or a reflection. Find some appropriate way to bring the group from the workaday world into a sacred time of graced sharing.

• If you have not been together before, name tags are very helpful as group members begin to become acquainted with one another.

• Spend the first session getting acquainted with one another, reading the Introduction aloud, and discussing the questions that follow.

• Appoint a group facilitator to provide guidance to the discussion. The role of facilitator may rotate among members each week. The facilitator simply keeps the discussion on track; each person shares responsibility for the group. There is no need for the facilitator to be a trained teacher.

• Try to study the six lessons on your own during the week. When you have done your own reflection and written your own answers, you will be better prepared to discuss the six scriptural lessons with the group. If you have not had an opportunity to study the passages during the week, meet with the group anyway to share support and insights.

• Participate in the discussion as much as you are able, offering your thoughts, insights, feelings, and decisions. You learn by sharing with others the fruits of your study.

• Be careful not to dominate the discussion. It is important that everyone in the group be offered an equal opportunity to share the results of their work. Try to link what you say to the comments of others so that the group remains on the topic.

• When discussing your own personal thoughts or feelings, use "I" language. Be as personal and honest as appropriate, and be very cautious about giving advice to others.

• Listen attentively to the other members of the group so as to learn from their insights. The words of the Bible affect each person in a different way, so a group provides a wealth of understanding for each member.

• Don't fear silence. Silence in a group is as important as silence in personal study. It allows individuals time to listen to the voice of God's Spirit and the opportunity to form their thoughts before they speak.

• Solicit several responses for each question. The thoughts of different people will build on the answers of others and will lead to deeper insights for all.

• Don't fear controversy. Differences of opinions are a sign of a healthy and honest group. If you cannot resolve an issue, continue on, agreeing to disagree. There is probably some truth in each viewpoint.

• Discuss the questions that seem most important for the group. There is no need to cover all the questions in the group session.

• Realize that some questions about the Bible cannot be resolved, even by experts. Don't get stuck on some issue for which there are no clear answers.

• Whatever is said in the group is said in confidence and should be regarded as such.

• Pray as a group in whatever way feels comfortable. Pray for the members of your group throughout the week.

Schedule for Group Study

Session 1: Introduction   Date: _____

Session 2: Lessons 1–6   Date: _____

Session 3: Lessons 7–12   Date: _____

Session 4: Lessons 13–18   Date: _____

Session 5: Lessons 19–24   Date: _____

Session 6: Lessons 25–30   Date: _____

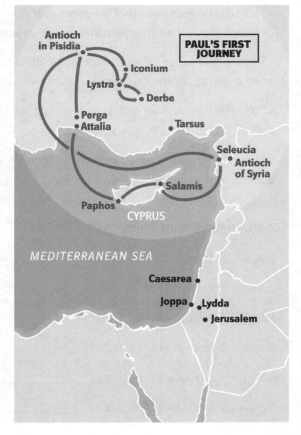

PAUL'S FIRST JOURNEY

Antioch in Pisidia

Iconium

Lystra

Derbe

Perga

Attalia

Tarsus

Seleucia

Antioch of Syria

Salamis

Paphos

CYPRUS

MEDITERRANEAN SEA

Caesarea

Joppa

Lydda

Jerusalem

"You will receive power when the Holy Spirit has come upon you; and you will be my witnesses in Jerusalem, in all Judea and Samaria, and to the ends of the earth." Acts 1:8

Church of the Holy Spirit (Part 1)

The Bible is full of adventure, but the Acts of the Apostles is perhaps the most adventurous book of all. It takes us to some of the great cities of the ancient world: to holy Jerusalem, wealthy Antioch, scholarly Athens, cosmopolitan Corinth, and powerful Rome. It introduces us to all kinds of people: apostles, prophets, martyrs, philosophers, governors, kings, merchants, jailers, and sailors. It narrates for us a variety of events: dramatic spiritual experiences, missionary journeys, trials and imprisonments, powerful speeches that provoke dramatic responses, sea voyages and a shipwreck, and the clash of ancient cultures.

This work is most thrilling because here we see Christianity in its earliest youth, being lived for the first time in history. But we don't just read about these historical events as objective observers. As members of this same church, we are invited into this adventurous story because we realize in its telling that the adventure continues into the lives of all those who claim to be followers of Jesus Christ. The book of Acts is open-ended, for it continues into the life of the church and its members in every age.

The Acts of the Apostles is the second volume of a two-part work; the first volume is the Gospel according to Luke. The gospel is the account of Jesus, from his birth to his eternally glorified presence in heaven; Acts is the account of the early church, from its birth at Pentecost to its extended presence reaching out to the whole world. Yet, Jesus is the center of both works. In the first volume he is visibly present; in the second, he is the "absent" Lord who continues to work powerfully in the world through his word and his Spirit. In Acts, Jesus is not a hero from the past; he is the Lord of the present. Though established in his heavenly abode, Jesus continues to be present to his community on earth, empowering mediators to act on his behalf to continue the mission he began.

Luke must have drawn from a variety of earlier sources to write the Acts of the Apostles, just as he drew from several sources for his gospel. There were probably accounts, both oral and written, about the individual heroes of the early church—Peter, John, Stephen, Philip. There must have been collected records of local churches—Antioch, Corinth, Caesarea, Ephesus, and Jerusalem—from which Luke gathered details of events in those places. Perhaps Luke had access to travel diaries written by those who accompanied Paul. It is quite possible that Luke knew some of the influential people from the early churches—people like Barnabas, Timothy, Silas, Philip, Mark, Aquila and Priscilla, and even Paul himself—from whom he collected material for his detailed account of the apostolic church.

There was no shortage of informants and it was probably a case of too much information rather than too little. Luke had to decide what to leave out and what to put in. If we think about all that Luke could have written, we might get frustrated at how little he really tells us. There is much that we would like to know that Luke did not include. We might think that the book was misnamed: for it tells us almost nothing about most of the original twelve apostles, except for a list of their names in 1:13. We read a lot about Peter, and a little about John, James, and Judas, but that is all. Instead, we are introduced to lots of characters who are not apostles. We read about how the church expanded westward, through Greece and into Rome. But we are told nothing about the growth of the church in other directions—south into Egypt or east into Arabia. We certainly would have wanted to read a complete account of the lives of Peter and Paul. We see the deeds of Peter in the first half of Acts, but then we don't read any more about him. The life of Paul seems complete as we read, but the book ends with Paul as a prisoner in Rome. The book is left open-ended and seems incomplete.

Acts is the only book we have that narrates the church's earliest history. If Acts had been lost, there is no work that could have taken its place. There are a few hints of events in the early church in Paul's letters, but they do not give us the information we would long to know. What happened to the followers of Jesus? What did they do next? What did they do with the teachings of Jesus and the commission he gave them to continue his work? Without Acts there would be a gaping chasm in the New Testament, with the gospels on one side and the letters on the other. Acts is the necessary link, pulling the New Testament into a complete collection of inspired literature.

Reflection and discussion

• What motivates you to want to study the Acts of the Apostles?

• What might be some of the reasons why Acts seems incomplete and open-ended?

The Holy Spirit as Guide and Inspiration for the Church

The Acts of the Apostles might more accurately be called the Acts of the Holy Spirit. It is this Spirit of God who is the truest apostle—"the one who is sent" by God to empower and guide the early church. In his narrative, Luke traces the way the Spirit of God guided the community of disciples from the beginning of the church throughout the early stages of its growth. This same Holy Spirit, we may presume from Acts, continues to direct the church which had its origin at Pentecost and is now two thousand years old.

Luke's description of God's saving plan is marked out in three stages: that of Israel, of Jesus, and of the church. Both Luke's gospel and Acts begin with a transition to a new stage, and both of those transition periods are directed by the Holy Spirit. The birth and infancy narratives at the beginning of Luke's gospel mark the transition from the epoch of Israel to the new age of Jesus. And the birth and early days of the church at the beginning of Acts mark the transition to the new stage of the church.

After the age of Israel in which God's Spirit was diffuse, being bestowed periodically by God to his chosen prophets, priests, and kings, Jesus is uniquely and profusely blessed by the Spirit. This divine Spirit is the agent of God's action in Jesus throughout his life and the dynamism of his ministry. Jesus does not pass on the Spirit until his earthly mission is complete. But following his resurrection and ascension into glory, he bestows his Spirit permanently within his church. Once this community of disciples receives the Spirit, it is able to act as Jesus did. The Spirit that was his alone is now poured out upon them all. Peter proclaims: "having received from the Father the promise of the Holy Spirit, [Jesus] has poured out this that you both see and hear" (2:33). "Clothed with power from on high" (Luke 24:49), the community will now minister the presence of Jesus as Lord in the world. From the time of Pentecost, all the major characters in Acts are driven by the Spirit to act courageously and preach boldly. Clearly Luke considers the Holy Spirit to be the "life-principle" of the church.

The Holy Spirit guided the mission of the early church according to God's designs. In what has been called a "triple Pentecost," Luke narrates the gift of the Spirit first to the Jews, then to the Samaritans, and finally to the Gentiles. In the first Pentecost, many Jewish people gathered in Jerusalem accepted Peter's invitation to repent, be baptized, and receive the Holy Spirit (Acts 2:38). As Luke narrates the witness of Jesus' disciples expanding to Judea and Samaria, he shows us that many Samaritans began accepting the word of God. So the apostles sent Peter and John to pray for the Spirit with the Samaritans, and they "laid their hands on them and they received the Holy Spirit" (8:17). The final expansion of the good news to non-Jews—the Gentiles—began in the city of Caesarea. When Peter was speaking to the crowd, he proclaimed that "God shows no partiality" (10:34)—that people from any nation can experience God's salvation. While he was speaking, "the Holy Spirit fell upon all who heard the word." The Jews who had accompanied Peter were amazed that "the gift of the Holy Spirit had been poured out even on the Gentiles" (10:44-45). This third outpouring of God's Spirit indicated that both Jews and Gentiles could be equally endowed with the gift of the Holy Spirit, thus making way for the expansion of the Christian mission to the whole world. Thus, the Holy Spirit guided the Christian mission, first in Jerusalem, then into Judea and Samaria, and finally to the ends of the earth (1:8). The Spirit drove the church to cross every barrier in proclaiming the gospel.

Reflection and discussion

• In what ways does Luke show that the Holy Spirit is the life-principle of the early church?

• What does the Holy Spirit encourage the community of disciples to do? How might God's Spirit be encouraging me as I begin this study of Acts?

God's Salvation Extended to All

The entire event of Jesus Christ, from his earthly ministry through the expansion of his ministry in his church, is framed by the theme of the salvation of

God. The life of Jesus is prefaced by the proclamation that "all flesh shall see the salvation of God" (Luke 3:6), and Acts concludes with the announcement that "this salvation of God has been sent to the Gentiles" (Acts 28:28). Jesus was proclaimed as Savior by the angels at his birth, and both Peter and Paul announce that Jesus is Savior for Israel (Acts 5:31; 13:23). By applying this ancient title for God to Jesus himself, Luke assures us that God has brought salvation to the world in Jesus.

God's whole plan for the world can be described as the history of salvation. This divine plan had been revealed by God in the Hebrew Scriptures, and the events recorded in Luke and Acts are the completion of God's ancient plan. At the end of the gospel, Jesus told his disciples "that everything written about me in the law of Moses, the prophets, and the psalms must be fulfilled" (Luke 24:44). Acts confirms that the Scriptures of Israel are fulfilled in Jesus (Acts 1:16; 3:18-25). Luke stresses the continuity of God's plan, which was worked out through the history of Israel, of Jesus, and of the church. Jesus is the center of God's plan; he unites the past, present, and future. He is the one who was promised in the Hebrew Scriptures and who brought salvation through his life, death, and resurrection. And it is Jesus who continues after his resurrection and ascension to offer salvation to all humanity through his representatives in the early church. Indeed, "there is salvation in no one else, for there is no other name under heaven given among mortals by which we must be saved" (Acts 4:12). The bestowal of the Spirit on both Jews and Gentiles demonstrates that God treats everyone the same, gives the same opportunities to all, and calls upon all people to respond to the salvation he offers through Jesus Christ.

Through the Holy Spirit, God unites Jesus and his church. Luke demonstrates this unity and continuity by showing parallels between Jesus and the apostolic community and between his gospel and Acts. The divine Spirit comes down on the assembled community at Pentecost, dwelling within the disciples and empowering the church, just as the empowering Spirit came to dwell in Jesus at his baptism. As Jesus had an introductory speech setting forth the purpose of his mission (Luke 4), so do his disciples, Peter and Paul (Acts 2:14f; 13:16f). As Jesus raised men and women from the dead (Luke 7:11-17; 8:40-56), so do Peter and Paul in the raising of Tabitha and Eutychus (Acts 9:36-43; 20:7-12). The trials of Jesus have intriguing parallels in the trial scenes of Stephen and Paul in Acts. The farewell discourse of Jesus in Luke 21 parallels the farewell discourse of Paul at Miletus in Acts 20.

These many parallels are the author's way of demonstrating that the life of Jesus continues in his church: like master, like disciple. As Jesus prayed, preached, taught, healed, reconciled, and suffered, so his followers are shown doing the same things. We are invited into this ongoing account as disciples of Jesus. We too are called to do as Jesus did, to be his living presence in the world. This open-ended history continues in the lives of all who receive the "Spirit of Jesus" (16:7), in the lives of people ready to believe, pray, teach, serve, and forgive.

Reflection and discussion

• What does God's salvation mean to me? What does it mean to say that Jesus is the Savior of the world?

• What are some of the ways that Luke shows the role of the church in extending God's salvation to the world?

The Call to Evangelize the World

God's desire to bring salvation to the world means that God wants all people everywhere to experience the forgiveness and divine life offered through Jesus Christ. Acts presents this universal will of God by demonstrating the world-wide mission of the church. By filling his gospel with outcasts and marginalized people, Luke began to teach his readers that they are to be witnesses to all people. All kinds of people are the recipients of the mission of Jesus: rich and poor, powerful and weak, men and women, sinners and saints. In Acts we see a further extension of that mission: to widows, centurions, merchants, jailers, philosophers, governors, kings, and sailors. The gospel reaches into the lives of every imaginable kind of person. Disciples of Jesus are to be witnesses to every person throughout the world.

In the programmatic verse of Acts, Jesus commissions his apostles to be witnesses, first "in Jerusalem," then "in all Judea and Samaria," and finally "to the ends of the earth" (1:8). This opening-out of the gospel message to a continually wider audience forms the structure of the book. The good news of forgiveness and the manifestation of God's Spirit is offered first to the Jews in Jerusalem, but then to "all who are far away, everyone whom the Lord our God calls to him" (2:39).

Beyond Jerusalem, the good news is first spread to the Samaritans (8:4-13). Then the message of salvation is offered to an Ethiopian traveling in Judea (8:26-39). It is then brought to the coastal region, to the inhabitants of Lydda, Sharon, and Joppa (9:31-43). The outreach to the Gentiles, the clearest expression of the church's universal mission, begins with Peter's entering the home of Cornelius and the conversion of his household. The Gentile mission is then followed by the mission to the Greeks in Antioch, and then by the long journeys of Paul with his fellow missionaries. The journeys of Paul extend throughout Asia Minor, into Greece, and finally to the capital of the empire, the city of Rome. When Paul travels to Rome, his witness to Christ has truly become universal; the mission has extended "to all the nations."

This extension of salvation to the Gentiles does not mean that God has taken back his promises to Israel. Luke struggles with the fact that the majority of Jews did not come to believe in Jesus as the Messiah, yet he never gave up on the "hope of Israel" (28:20). Luke makes it clear that thousands of Jews in Jerusalem converted in response to the apostles' preaching (2:41; 4:4). The Jewish-Christian community grows steadily in number as more and more Jews join the community of believers (5:14; 6:7). Before showing the mission of Paul to convert the Gentiles, Luke wants to show us that God is faithful to his own historical people. Yet, even for Paul, the apostle to the Gentiles, the mission to the Jews is primary. Consistently Paul goes first to the synagogue of each town and preaches to the Jews. Even when his message is rejected there and Paul states that he is turning to the Gentiles, he never gives up on his fellow Jews. Even the final scene of Acts shows Paul preaching the message of salvation, "from the law of Moses and the prophets" (28:23), to the Jewish people of Rome. Luke reports that "some were convinced by what he had said, while others refused to believe" (28:24).

Acts presents for us a church made up of all kinds of people: Jews and Gentiles, the alienated and outcasts, apostles and martyrs. From Jerusalem to Rome, the people of God grow in number and devotion, accepting the gift of salvation which is offered to all. The community of those "saved through the grace of the Lord Jesus" (15:11) is destined to spread to the ends of the earth.

Reflection and discussion

• In what way does the programmatic verse at the beginning of Acts (1:8) outline the entire scope of the book and the church's mission?

• How does my own life seem to fit into God's saving plan for the world?

Prayer

Lord God, you raised up Luke to receive the gospel of Jesus Christ and to evangelize through his writing the Acts of the Apostles. Prepare my heart to experience the dynamic presence of the Holy Spirit through the pages of this inspired work. Show me how to take these words to heart and to meditate upon them. Stir up within me a deep desire to respond to the Spirit's promptings and guidance as I seek to follow the way of Jesus in the world. Keep me faithful these weeks to the challenges of study and prayer which your word offers to me.

SUGGESTIONS FOR FACILITATORS, GROUP SESSION 1

1. If the group is meeting for the first time, or if there are newcomers joining the group, it is helpful to provide nametags.

2. Distribute the books to the members of the group.

3. You may want to ask the participants to introduce themselves and tell the group a bit about themselves.

4. Ask one or more of these introductory questions:
   - What drew you to join this group?
   - What is your biggest fear in beginning this Bible study?
   - How is beginning this study like a "threshold" for you?

5. You may want to pray this prayer as a group:

   Come upon us, Holy Spirit, to enlighten and guide us as we begin this study of the Acts of the Apostles. You inspired the writers of the Scriptures to reveal your presence throughout the history of salvation. This inspired word has the power to convert our hearts and change our lives. Fill our hearts with desire, trust, and confidence as you shine the light of your truth within us. Motivate us to read the Scriptures, and give us a deeper love for God's word each day. Bless us during this session and throughout the coming week with the fire of your love.

6. Read the Introduction aloud, pausing at each question for discussion. Group members may wish to write the insights of the group as each question is discussed. Encourage several members of the group to respond to each question.

7. Don't feel compelled to finish the complete Introduction during the session. It is better to allow sufficient time to talk about the questions raised than to rush to the end. Group members may read any remaining sections on their own after the group meeting.

8. Instruct group members to read the first six lessons on their own during the six days before the next group meeting. They should write out their own answers to the questions as preparation for next week's group discussion.

9. Fill in the date for each group meeting under "Schedule for Group Study."

10. Conclude the session by praying aloud together the prayer at the end of the Introduction.

"Men of Galilee, why do you stand looking up toward heaven?
This Jesus, who has been taken up from you into heaven,
will come in the same way as you saw him go into heaven." Acts 1:11

Jesus Gives a Mission to His Church

ACTS 1:1-11 *¹In the first book, Theophilus, I wrote about all that Jesus did and taught from the beginning ²until the day when he was taken up to heaven, after giving instructions through the Holy Spirit to the apostles whom he had chosen. ³After his suffering he presented himself alive to them by many convincing proofs, appearing to them during forty days and speaking about the kingdom of God. ⁴While staying with them, he ordered them not to leave Jerusalem, but to wait there for the promise of the Father. "This," he said, "is what you have heard from me; ⁵for John baptized with water, but you will be baptized with the Holy Spirit not many days from now."*

⁶So when they had come together, they asked him, "Lord, is this the time when you will restore the kingdom to Israel?" ⁷He replied, "It is not for you to know the times or periods that the Father has set by his own authority. ⁸But you will receive power when the Holy Spirit has come upon you; and you will be my witnesses in Jerusalem, in all Judea and Samaria, and to the ends of the earth." ⁹When he had said this, as they were watching, he was lifted up, and a cloud took him out of their sight. ¹⁰While he was going and they were gazing up toward heaven, suddenly two men in white robes stood by them. ¹¹They said, "Men of

Galilee, why do you stand looking up toward heaven? This Jesus, who has been taken up from you into heaven, will come in the same way as you saw him go into heaven."

In order to move on to his second volume, Luke summarizes the content of "the first book," the Gospel according to Luke (verse 1). "All that Jesus did and taught"—his choosing of apostles, his suffering and resurrection appearances, his commission that they be witnesses to the world, the promise of the Spirit, and his ascension into heaven—forms a transition to the new stage of history, the story of the church. In his gospel, Luke had demonstrated that all the activities of Jesus were directed by the Holy Spirit, through whom Jesus had been conceived and by whom he had been anointed. In Acts, Luke shows that the church is empowered and directed by the same Holy Spirit, through whom the church is conceived and in whom the church is baptized and anointed. Truly, this two-volume work is united through the dynamic action of the Holy Spirit.

When the disciples meet with the risen Jesus, they are filled with hope and yearning. They want Jesus to finish the work he has begun, to fulfill his promise to restore God's kingdom (verse 6). The reply of Jesus is twofold: first, he tells them that they cannot know "the times or periods that the Father has set," ending their speculation about the end of the age (verse 7); and second, he tells them that they will be his "witnesses" in the world (verse 8). The promised kingdom will be fully restored as a gift in God's own time. In the meantime, they are not to wait idly; rather, they are to be witnesses filled with hope in the promises Jesus has left them.

The ascension of Jesus means that the disciples' understanding of the world is now different. They recognize that the one who has taught, healed, and loved them has been raised to rule with the world's Creator. In this new reality, the future is still to be fully realized; it is open-ended to the movements of God's Spirit. The disciples are not to stand gazing up toward heaven, for the presence of Jesus will be with them in the spiritual outpouring they will soon receive. They should return to Jerusalem to await their empowerment by the Holy Spirit for their witness, because the same Spirit who empowered Jesus will be present in his church.

The two great figures of the Torah and the prophets, Moses and Elijah, each transmitted their "spirit" to their successors at their departure. Because Moses laid his hands on Joshua, his successor, Joshua was filled with the spirit of wisdom and did as God had commanded Moses (Deut 34:9). Before Elijah ascended into heaven, Elisha, his successor, asked for a double share of his spirit. So when Elijah departed, his spirit was actively present in his successor (2 Kings 2:9, 15). Likewise, as Jesus departs, he promises his Spirit to his disciples. In fact, the two men in white garments may well represent Moses and Elijah, the departed predecessors of Jesus, who appeared with him at the Transfiguration (verse 10). Jesus could have stayed on earth longer, or even forever, but he departed in order to leave his work in the hands of his church. The entire book of Acts demonstrates, then, that the work of Jesus continues in the church through the power of the Holy Spirit.

Reflection and discussion

• Do I seek Jesus by gazing to heaven or by doing his work on earth? What part of his mission has Jesus entrusted to me?

• What are the indicators that Luke's gospel continues in Acts? How is the Holy Spirit the power who unites the two parts of Luke's work?

• What is the task of disciples between the time of Jesus' ascension and his return in glory? Why does Jesus tell them not to speculate about the future? Why do the men in white tell them not to remain looking heavenward?

• Both Moses and Elijah ended their work on earth by passing on their own spirit to their successors. In what sense does Jesus complete this pattern?

• How does the beginning of Acts confirm, modify, or overturn my understanding of the purpose and mission of the church?

Prayer

Ascended Lord, send your Holy Spirit to me so that I may understand your word and proclaim it through my life. Empower me to witness to you and to continue your work in the world today. Come, Holy Spirit, come.

All these were constantly devoting themselves to prayer,
together with certain women, including Mary the mother of Jesus,
as well as his brothers. Acts 1:14

Reestablishing the Twelve Apostles

ACTS 1:12-26 *¹²Then they returned to Jerusalem from the mount called Olivet, which is near Jerusalem, a sabbath day's journey away. ¹³When they had entered the city, they went to the room upstairs where they were staying, Peter, and John, and James, and Andrew, Philip and Thomas, Bartholomew and Matthew, James son of Alphaeus, and Simon the Zealot, and Judas son of James. ¹⁴All these were constantly devoting themselves to prayer, together with certain women, including Mary the mother of Jesus, as well as his brothers.*

¹⁵In those days Peter stood up among the believers (together the crowd numbered about one hundred twenty persons) and said, ¹⁶"Friends, the scripture had to be fulfilled, which the Holy Spirit through David foretold concerning Judas, who became a guide for those who arrested Jesus—¹⁷for he was numbered among us and was allotted his share in this ministry." ¹⁸(Now this man acquired a field with the reward of his wickedness; and falling headlong, he burst open in the middle and all his bowels gushed out. ¹⁹This became known to all the residents of Jerusalem, so that the field was called in their language Hakeldama, that is, Field of Blood.) ²⁰"For it is written in the book of Psalms,

'Let his homestead become desolate,

and let there be no one to live in it';
and
'Let another take his position of overseer.'

[21]So one of the men who have accompanied us during all the time that the Lord Jesus went in and out among us, [22]beginning from the baptism of John until the day when he was taken up from us—one of these must become a witness with us to his resurrection." [23]So they proposed two, Joseph called Barsabbas, who was also known as Justus, and Matthias. [24]Then they prayed and said, "Lord, you know everyone's heart. Show us which one of these two you have chosen [25]to take the place in this ministry and apostleship from which Judas turned aside to go to his own place." [26]And they cast lots for them, and the lot fell on Matthias; and he was added to the eleven apostles.

The apostles travel the short distance over the steep descent from Mount Olivet and the equally steep ascent back into the city of Jerusalem. They return to the upper room where they had shared in the last supper of Jesus. Those gathered there had experienced the entire ministry of Jesus, including his crucifixion and resurrection appearances. The eleven apostles are joined with Mary the mother of Jesus, some of the women who had followed Jesus from Galilee, and some of Jesus' extended family (verse 14). This is the nucleus of the church that will be empowered for mission by the Father's gift of the Spirit. This time between the ascension and Pentecost is a significant pause between God's mighty acts, a pause in which the church's task is to wait and pray, "Come, Holy Spirit." The witness of disciples must be more than just earnest striving and busy activity. They must await God's grace with expectant hearts. Waiting and praying teach us that God's gift of the Spirit is never our assured possession. God's Spirit must be constantly sought anew in prayer.

The scene mirrors the beginning of Luke's first volume. The gospel begins with the coming of the Holy Spirit upon Mary, the mother of Jesus, in order to give birth to Israel's Savior. Acts begins with the coming of the Holy Spirit upon Mary and the apostles, in order to give birth to the church. As with Jesus, who was filled with the Holy Spirit throughout his saving mission on earth, the church will be filled with the Holy Spirit for its expanding mission in the world. Throughout Luke's inspired writing, Mary is a model for the kind of expectant faith in God's promises which Jesus desires for his church: "Blessed is she who believed that there would be a fulfillment of what was spoken to her by the Lord" (Luke 1:45).

As the apostles wait in Jerusalem for the coming of the Spirit, they discern through prayer and Scripture that they should choose another to complete the number of the twelve apostles. The betrayal of Judas and his ultimate suicide left a gap that must be filled before the Spirit descends to empower the apostolic church. Someone must take his office of responsibility within the core circle of apostles. The choice of an apostle is made this time, not by Jesus, but by those who will continue his work. The Twelve must be reconstituted before Pentecost, so that in that event Israel will be restored as the people of God.

Peter addresses the community about the process for replacing Judas. He states that the candidate must be "one of the men who have accompanied us throughout the time that the Lord Jesus went in and out among us" (verse 21). This span of witness includes the entire time of Jesus' ministry and teaching, from the baptizing of John to the ascension of Jesus. The unique qualifications of this office demonstrate its foundational role for the church. Two men are put forward for the apostolic ministry: Barsabbas and Matthias. Accompanied by the prayer of the community, the final choice is left to God. Through the casting of lots, the Lord's choice of Matthias is made clear. The decision is made both on qualifications and on divine choice. It is made from below, from the ranks of those whom the prayerful community chooses, and from above, as God graciously guides his church to fulfill its mission.

Matthias is then counted with the eleven apostles and the number is restored to twelve. The twelve apostles link the church to the events which originated the church, and through their "witness to the resurrection" they lead the church to fulfill its mission. With Peter, they testify to what has happened so that it may continue to happen within the church. With the twelve apostles restored, the community is ready for the coming of the Holy Spirit.

Reflection and discussion

• In what ways is Mary a model for the newly emerging church?

• Why is waiting and praying just as important for the church as projects and activities?

• Peter describes the passage which he quotes from the book of Psalms as a revelation from God, that is, as Scripture "which the Holy Spirit through David foretold." In what ways does this description of Scripture imply both its divine and human origins?

• The process for replacing Judas among the twelve apostles forms a precedent for how to make decisions as a community, looking to God to show the way. What elements of this process of discernment can help the church make decisions today?

Prayer

Come, Holy Spirit, teach me how to wait and pray for the experience of your outpouring. Transform me with your grace and make me holy so that I may bear witness to the name of Jesus through what I say and do. Help me to await Christ's return with joyful hope.

All of them were filled with the Holy Spirit and began to speak in other languages, as the Spirit gave them ability. Acts 2:4

The Gift of the Holy Spirit

ACTS 2:1-21 *¹When the day of Pentecost had come, they were all together in one place. ²And suddenly from heaven there came a sound like the rush of a violent wind, and it filled the entire house where they were sitting. ³Divided tongues, as of fire, appeared among them, and a tongue rested on each of them. ⁴All of them were filled with the Holy Spirit and began to speak in other languages, as the Spirit gave them ability.*

⁵Now there were devout Jews from every nation under heaven living in Jerusalem. ⁶And at this sound the crowd gathered and was bewildered, because each one heard them speaking in the native language of each. ⁷Amazed and astonished, they asked, "Are not all these who are speaking Galileans? ⁸And how is it that we hear, each of us, in our own native language? ⁹Parthians, Medes, Elamites, and residents of Mesopotamia, Judea and Cappadocia, Pontus and Asia, ¹⁰Phrygia and Pamphylia, Egypt and the parts of Libya belonging to Cyrene, and visitors from Rome, both Jews and proselytes, ¹¹Cretans and

Arabs—in our own languages we hear them speaking about God's deeds of power." [12]*All were amazed and perplexed, saying to one another, "What does this mean?"* [13]*But others sneered and said, "They are filled with new wine."*

[14]*But Peter, standing with the eleven, raised his voice and addressed them, "Men of Judea and all who live in Jerusalem, let this be known to you, and listen to what I say.* [15]*Indeed, these are not drunk, as you suppose, for it is only nine o'clock in the morning.* [16]*No, this is what was spoken through the prophet Joel:*

[17]*'In the last days it will be, God declares,*
that I will pour out my Spirit upon all flesh,
  and your sons and your daughters shall prophesy,
and your young men shall see visions,
  and your old men shall dream dreams.
[18]*Even upon my slaves, both men and women,*
  in those days I will pour out my Spirit;
  and they shall prophesy.
[19]*And I will show portents in the heaven above*
  and signs on the earth below,
    blood, and fire, and smoky mist.
[20]*The sun shall be turned to darkness*
  and the moon to blood,
    before the coming of the Lord's great and glorious day.
[21]*Then everyone who calls on the name of the Lord shall be saved.'"*

The great event of Pentecost, in which the church burst forth with divine life, is narrated in only four verses (verses 1-4). But the truest significance of that event is the empowerment of the disciples by the Holy Spirit, and the result of that event continues throughout Acts and into the third millennium. John the Baptist had foretold that Jesus would baptize "with the Holy Spirit and fire" (Luke 3:16), and Jesus had said, "I came to bring fire to the earth, and how I wish it were already kindled!" (Luke 12:49). Now the baptism of the church with the Spirit and fire stirs into flame the grace of Christ's death and resurrection and breathes divine power into the newborn church.

The Jewish feast of Weeks/Pentecost, celebrated as a pilgrimage festival in Jerusalem, came to be associated with the giving of the Torah on Mount Sinai as a covenant-making event. In Exodus, God established the covenant with Israel at Mount Sinai and claimed them as his own people. In Acts, God creates the church and completes his promises to Israel as they renew the covenant at Pentecost. At Sinai, God came down upon the mountain with a terrifying noise and in a mysterious fire (Exod 19:16-19). The great sound and fire of Pentecost signify the mysterious presence of God that fills and renews God's people with his Spirit.

The coming of the Holy Spirit takes place in the presence of Jews on pilgrimage from all around the world. Luke's writing establishes a parallel between the coming of the Spirit upon Jesus at his baptism (Luke 3:21-22) and the coming of the Spirit on the apostles. Immediately after the Spirit descended on Jesus, Luke listed the generations of Jews from Jesus back to Abraham and even further to Adam (Luke 3:23-38). After the Spirit descended upon those who would continue the work of Jesus, Luke lists all the nations around the world from which the Jews have gathered (verses 5-11). The church begins with the Jewish apostles of Jesus announcing the good news to Jewish people from throughout the world. The Twelve are the nucleus of God's restored people, and the audience asks the question that will be answered in the coming chapters: "What does this mean?" (verse 12).

Not only is God creating his people anew, but the Spirit is coming to rest on each person as they begin to speak fearlessly. The very first person to speak is Peter. The same spirit that God blew into the dust to create a human being (Gen 2:7) now breathes life into this once cowardly disciple to create a new man. The same Peter who only a few weeks before could not speak up when his master was on trial now proclaims the message of Christ in the power of the Holy Spirit (verse 14).

Peter's proclamation from the prophet Joel indicates that God's promises were being fulfilled as the Holy Spirit is poured out without measure (verses 17-18). In previous ages, the Spirit had been given in measured form to prophets, priests, and kings. Now, through the saving death and resurrection of God's Messiah, all God's people experience the manifestation of God's Spirit—sons and daughters, men and women, young and old, slaves and free people. What Moses had longed for is now a reality: "Would that all the Lord's people were prophets, and that the Lord would put his spirit on them!" (Num 11:29). Now all God's people share in the prophetic, priestly, and kingly anointing of Christ through sharing in his Spirit.

Reflection and discussion

• The Holy Spirit still blows through the world, searching for hearts willing to be transformed by grace. What wonders is the Spirit displaying in the world today? What fire of grace do I wish to be lit in my heart?

• In what ways was Peter affected by the power of the Holy Spirit? In what similar ways has God's Spirit transformed my life?

• What is the relationship between the feasts of the Annunciation, the Baptism of Jesus, and Pentecost? Why is Pentecost the conclusion of the liturgical season of Easter?

Prayer

Creator God, you send your Spirit to complete your creative work in me. Take away my timid and cowardly spirit and give me a spirit of courage and fervor. Sanctify my heart for the glory of your kingdom, and kindle in me the fire of your divine love.

"Repent, and be baptized every one of you in the name of Jesus Christ so that your sins may be forgiven; and you will receive the gift of the Holy Spirit." Acts 2:38

The Crucified Jesus
Is Lord and Messiah

ACTS 2:22-47 *22"You that are Israelites, listen to what I have to say: Jesus of Nazareth, a man attested to you by God with deeds of power, wonders, and signs that God did through him among you, as you yourselves know—23this man, handed over to you according to the definite plan and foreknowledge of God, you crucified and killed by the hands of those outside the law. 24But God raised him up, having freed him from death, because it was impossible for him to be held in its power. 25For David says concerning him,*

'I saw the Lord always before me,
  for he is at my right hand so that I will not be shaken;
26therefore my heart was glad, and my tongue rejoiced;
  moreover my flesh will live in hope.
27For you will not abandon my soul to Hades,
  or let your Holy One experience corruption.
28You have made known to me the ways of life;
  you will make me full of gladness with your presence.'

  29"Fellow Israelites, I may say to you confidently of our ancestor David that he both died and was buried, and his tomb is with us to this day. 30Since he was a

23

prophet, he knew that God had sworn with an oath to him that he would put one of his descendants on his throne. [31]Foreseeing this, David spoke of the resurrection of the Messiah, saying,

'He was not abandoned to Hades,
   nor did his flesh experience corruption.'

[32]This Jesus God raised up, and of that all of us are witnesses. [33]Being therefore exalted at the right hand of God, and having received from the Father the promise of the Holy Spirit, he has poured out this that you both see and hear. [34]For David did not ascend into the heavens, but he himself says,

'The Lord said to my Lord,
"Sit at my right hand,
   [35]until I make your enemies your footstool."'

[36]Therefore let the entire house of Israel know with certainty that God has made him both Lord and Messiah, this Jesus whom you crucified."

[37]Now when they heard this, they were cut to the heart and said to Peter and to the other apostles, "Brothers, what should we do?" [38]Peter said to them, "Repent, and be baptized every one of you in the name of Jesus Christ so that your sins may be forgiven; and you will receive the gift of the Holy Spirit. [39]For the promise is for you, for your children, and for all who are far away, everyone whom the Lord our God calls to him." [40]And he testified with many other arguments and exhorted them, saying, "Save yourselves from this corrupt generation." [41]So those who welcomed his message were baptized, and that day about three thousand persons were added. [42]They devoted themselves to the apostles' teaching and fellowship, to the breaking of bread and the prayers.

[43]Awe came upon everyone, because many wonders and signs were being done by the apostles.[44]All who believed were together and had all things in common; [45]they would sell their possessions and goods and distribute the proceeds to all, as any had need. [46]Day by day, as they spent much time together in the temple, they broke bread at home and ate their food with glad and generous hearts, [47]praising God and having the goodwill of all the people. And day by day the Lord added to their number those who were being saved.

The speeches of the apostles, which are found throughout Acts, are replete with quotations from and allusions to the Scriptures of Israel. They express the early Christian interpretation of the Old Testament in light of the resurrection of Jesus, the key that opens up all the mysteries hidden in Israel's Scriptures. These speeches proclaim that Jesus is the climax of God's saving plan and that his life, death, and resurrection fulfill the ancient Scriptures.

This first sermon of Peter is an example of this apostolic preaching. Peter stands up with the other apostles and calls on the crowd to listen. He presents Jesus the Nazorean and proclaims what God has done through him. Even though he was crucified as a criminal in Jerusalem, his death was not an arbitrary tragedy; rather, he was "handed over to you according to the definite plan and foreknowledge of God." And God raised him from death, as his saving will directed, "because it was impossible for him to be held in its power" (verses 23-24). In this way, Peter expresses the necessity of the death and resurrection of Jesus in God's saving plan.

Many of the psalms of Israel can be read as referring either to King David or to his descendant, the Messiah. As evidence of this way of interpreting Scripture in light of the resurrection, Peter quotes a few verses from Psalm 16, a psalm of comfort. These words about the one who saw the Lord ever before him (verse 25), whose flesh will not experience corruption and whose soul is not abandoned to Hades (verses 26-27), and to whom God makes known the ways of life (verse 28), refer to the one who is risen and alive in the presence of God. They cannot refer to David: everyone knows he died and was buried; in fact, his tomb was still among them (verse 29). Rather, they proclaim David's descendent, Jesus the Messiah of Israel, the one who now reigns with God and pours forth his Spirit upon his church.

At the conclusion of Peter's speech, the people are cut to the heart when he accuses them of crucifying the one whom God has made "both Lord and Messiah" (verse 36). Many are provoked to ask, "What should we do?" Peter responds with a clear call for a decision involving a no and a yes: "Repent," saying no to your past life of rejecting God and living for yourselves, and "Be baptized," saying yes to God by faith in Jesus Christ. Through repentance and baptism, all who enter this new community receive forgiveness of sins and the gift of the Holy Spirit.

From his own bitter experience of denying Jesus and then experiencing forgiveness, Peter knows only too well what is needed to receive abundant life. Repentance is not just being sorry; it is an act of radical conversion of the mind and heart, a conscious turning toward God in order to receive the life he offers through Jesus. While repentance is primarily a personal and interior experience, baptism is a public and communal expression of this new life. Baptism "in the name of Jesus Christ" expresses one's faith in him and the reception of the gift of new life from God. God calls those in Jerusalem and their children as well as "all who are far away" to receive the gift of life he has promised. Many respond to Peter's exhortation with enthusiastic acceptance, and thousands are added to the community of faith. These form a powerful communal witness to others in the city, so that more and more people come to know Jesus as Messiah and Lord.

The resurrection of Jesus and the indwelling of the Holy Spirit truly transformed the lives of Jesus' followers. In a short summary we are offered a description of the early church in Jerusalem. Four elements characterize that to which they were continually devoted: the teaching of the apostles, the communal life, the breaking of bread, and the prayers. The fact that each of these four is specified by the definite article, "the," indicates that these are not just any teachings, fellowship, meals, and prayers. Rather, these are specific and particular actions of the early church.

The apostolic teaching includes doctrinal and ethical instructions rooted in the teachings of Jesus himself. As new members joined the community, they were offered these foundational teachings in order to deepen their understanding of the way of Jesus that they had chosen to follow. The communal life is more than just a warm-hearted fellowship among believers. The resurrection has truly transformed the priorities and social arrangements of their former status quo. Their unity in Christ extended to their sharing of material goods and a concern about all the needs of the community. The breaking of bread refers to the communal meals, including the Eucharist on the Lord's Day. Modeled on the meals Jesus shared during his life, culminating in the Last Supper, the believers continued to gather in homes to worship God, knowing that the Risen Jesus was with them in the breaking of the bread. The prayers are most likely fixed prayer in the morning and evening, in addition to spontaneous prayer for the needs of the church. They continued to attend the services of the temple, praying the psalms and prayers of their tradition. In addition, they developed liturgical prayers for their worship at table as well as hymns of praise and thanksgiving.

In essence, the believers formed a learning church, a loving church, a worshiping church, and an evangelizing church. The quality of their life together earned them the good favor of those outside the community. The church's witness was infectious, and their numbers steadily grew as God converted hearts and led many to salvation.

Reflection and discussion

• In what way is a decision about Jesus both a no and a yes? Why did so many respond enthusiastically to the message preached by Peter? Does the witness of my life add to the number of those being saved?

• Why does Peter's sermon include so many texts from the Psalms? How is my understanding amplified when I read the Psalms through, with, and in Jesus Christ?

• The communal life of the early church was a visible testimony and witness to their faith for those around them. How can a parish become a truly learning, loving, worshiping, and evangelizing church?

Prayer

Messiah and Lord, you continue to call people to repentance and baptism through the witness of your disciples. Empower me with your Spirit and form me as your witness today. Enkindle your church with the fire of the Holy Spirit.

"I have no silver or gold, but what I have I give you;
in the name of Jesus Christ of Nazareth, stand up and walk." Acts 3:6

The Lame Man Healed at the Temple Gate

ACTS 3:1-10 *¹One day Peter and John were going up to the temple at the hour of prayer, at three o'clock in the afternoon. ²And a man lame from birth was being carried in. People would lay him daily at the gate of the temple called the Beautiful Gate so that he could ask for alms from those entering the temple. ³When he saw Peter and John about to go into the temple, he asked them for alms. ⁴Peter looked intently at him, as did John, and said, "Look at us." ⁵And he fixed his attention on them, expecting to receive something from them. ⁶But Peter said, "I have no silver or gold, but what I have I give you; in the name of Jesus Christ of Nazareth, stand up and walk." ⁷And he took him by the right hand and raised him up; and immediately his feet and ankles were made strong. ⁸Jumping up, he stood and began to walk, and he entered the temple with them, walking and leaping and praising God. ⁹All the people saw him walking and praising God, ¹⁰and they recognized him as the one who used to sit and ask for alms at the Beautiful Gate of the temple; and they were filled with wonder and amazement at what had happened to him.*

T he work of the Spirit carries on where Jesus left off. The teaching, reconciling, and healing ministry of Jesus is extended into the life of the church through the Holy Spirit of Pentecost. The healing of the crippled beggar by Peter and John parallels the healing of the paralyzed man by Jesus in the gospel (Luke 5:17-26). Both accounts raise the issue of "what authority" is at work in the healing. The authority in each account is Jesus: Peter and John heal "in the name of Jesus Christ of Nazareth" (verse 6). It is as if Jesus was still with them, responding to the needs of the sick and afflicted people who came to him for help.

Every day for centuries, in the morning and afternoon, sacrifices had been offered in the temple. For years the man who had been lame from birth sat every day at the Beautiful Gate, one of the entrances into the area of the temple, to beg for alms. Since Peter and John regularly entered the temple for afternoon prayers, they must have known the man. Perhaps they had even given him coins, since offering alms was a responsibility that Judaism took seriously. But on this particular afternoon, the apostles "looked intently at him," sensing the Spirit's desire to intervene in the man's life. The lame man gives them his attention, no doubt hoping for financial help. Peter, however, provides him with more than money can buy. His words are emphatic and surprising: "I have no silver or gold, but what I have I give you; in the name of Jesus Christ of Nazareth, stand up and walk."

The miracle is not performed as a feat of magic to amaze the crowds. But, as in the healings of Jesus from the gospel, the miracle is a visual act that points to a deeper reality. In effect, Peter gives him a new life, portraying what God's salvation does in the life of all who receive it. In speaking of the salvation to come, the prophet Isaiah had said, "Then the eyes of the blind shall be opened, and the ears of the deaf unstopped; then the lame shall leap like a deer, and the tongue of the speechless sing for joy" (Isa 35:5-6). The lame man walking, leaping, and praising God is a tangible sign of the wholeness and fullness that salvation brings and that God desires for all people (verse 8).

This account shows how the emerging church is to engage the larger community in which it lives: demonstrating compassion in visible ways to manifest God's saving power. The healing brings "wonder and amazement" to those who recognize the healed man as the one who used to helplessly ask for alms at the temple gate. Such a response has the potential to both awaken faith and create controversy.

Reflection and discussion

• What is the difference between miracles and magic? Why was Peter able to work wonders in Jerusalem?

• Peter said: "I have neither silver nor gold, but what I do have I give you." What did Peter have to offer to the crippled man? Why did Peter choose to heal this lame man and not others?

• Every day God places someone in our path who is in need. What kinds of suffering and pain do I encounter most frequently in those around me? What can I do to bring healing to them?

Prayer

Lord Jesus, fill me with your Holy Spirit and heal those impediments that prevent me from serving you. Show me that I have more than silver and gold to offer, and teach me to be aware of the healing power that I possess in your name.

"His name itself has made this man strong, whom you see and know; and the faith that is through Jesus has given him this perfect health in the presence of all of you." Acts 3:16

Witness to Jesus in Solomon's Portico

ACTS 3:11-26 *¹¹While he clung to Peter and John, all the people ran together to them in the portico called Solomon's Portico, utterly astonished. ¹²When Peter saw it, he addressed the people, "You Israelites, why do you wonder at this, or why do you stare at us, as though by our own power or piety we had made him walk? ¹³The God of Abraham, the God of Isaac, and the God of Jacob, the God of our ancestors has glorified his servant Jesus, whom you handed over and rejected in the presence of Pilate, though he had decided to release him. ¹⁴But you rejected the Holy and Righteous One and asked to have a murderer given to you, ¹⁵and you killed the Author of life, whom God raised from the dead. To this we are witnesses. ¹⁶And by faith in his name, his name itself has made this man strong, whom you see and know; and the faith that is through Jesus has given him this perfect health in the presence of all of you.*

¹⁷"And now, friends, I know that you acted in ignorance, as did also your rulers. ¹⁸In this way God fulfilled what he had foretold through all the prophets, that his Messiah would suffer. ¹⁹Repent therefore, and turn to God so that your sins may be wiped out, ²⁰so that times of refreshing may come from the presence of the Lord, and that he may send the Messiah appointed for you, that is, Jesus,

²¹*who must remain in heaven until the time of universal restoration that God announced long ago through his holy prophets.* ²²*Moses said, 'The Lord your God will raise up for you from your own people a prophet like me. You must listen to whatever he tells you.* ²³*And it will be that everyone who does not listen to that prophet will be utterly rooted out of the people.'* ²⁴*And all the prophets, as many as have spoken, from Samuel and those after him, also predicted these days.* ²⁵*You are the descendants of the prophets and of the covenant that God gave to your ancestors, saying to Abraham, 'And in your descendants all the families of the earth shall be blessed.'* ²⁶*When God raised up his servant, he sent him first to you, to bless you by turning each of you from your wicked ways."*

Peter uses the opportunity of the crowd's amazement at the lame man's healing to focus their attention on Jesus Christ and to place the credit for the healing in the right place. The speech of Peter expresses the deeper meaning of the miracle account, and it establishes further parallels between Jesus and his apostles. Like Jesus, the apostles are now teaching in the area of the temple; and like Jesus, their teaching is closely connected to the amazing deeds they perform. The speech makes clear that the power at work in Peter and John is not their own. The crippled man was healed through faith in the risen Jesus.

Peter addresses his Jewish audience, speaking to them about the God of Abraham, Isaac, and Jacob (verse 13). Peter identifies himself as a member of God's people and a recipient of the promises of "the God of our ancestors" along with his audience. Peter wants to demonstrate that everything that God has done in his servant Jesus is the culmination of a long history of prophecy and expectation. Proclaiming how Jesus is the fulfillment of ancient Scriptures, Peter testifies to the significance of Jesus' death and resurrection. Jesus is the Messiah who suffered for his people, the Christ who fulfilled what God "foretold through all the prophets" (verse 18). He is "the Holy and Righteous One" who was rejected by those he came to save. Yet, their tragic denial and handing over of Jesus to death was met by God's raising him from the dead to become "the Author of life."

The final part of Peter's speech is a call to repentance and conversion (verse 19). Repentance means a change of mind, heart, and behavior; conversion means turning back to God. Peter admits that the religious leaders and the people of Jerusalem "acted in ignorance." Yet, ignorance does not leave them without responsibility. For this reason, Peter urges the crowd to repent and be converted. Their sin of not recognizing Jesus as the Messiah and of putting him to death can be forgiven. If they turn away from sin and toward God, their sins will be "wiped out." The Greek term also means "erased" or "obliterated" without leaving a trace, referring to what happened to letters written in ink when papyri were soaked and washed. As the letters on ancient scrolls were erased to create a new surface for writing, God wipes away sin through repentance and forgiveness.

The offer of blessings which God promised through Abraham and which is being proclaimed in the risen Lord is made to the people of Israel "first" (verses 25-26). But God offers healing and the opportunity of repentance to all people, "all the families of the earth." These gifts are possible for all because Jesus, "the Author of life," is risen from the dead. He alone has the power to restore people to their original wholeness and create them anew. Peter emphasizes life, not death; repentance, not blame; the forgiving power of God that can raise anyone from the death of sin, just as he raised Jesus from the grave.

Reflection and discussion

• What are the various titles of Jesus that Peter uses in his speech? Which of these titles holds the most significance for me?

• What might the healed man be thinking and feeling as he listened to Peter speak?

• As I listen to Peter's speech, which ideas move me to deeper faith?

• Peter urged his listeners to respond to the good news he preached by repentance and conversion. Why are repentance and conversion necessary in order to experience the forgiveness that God offers us?

• Peter told the crowd that, if they repent and be converted, their sins will be "wiped out." Do I believe that God completely erases my sins when I repent and turn to him?

Prayer

Jesus, you are God's Servant, the Holy and Righteous One, the Author of life, the Messiah of Israel, the Prophet like Moses, and the Lord of all. Give me the grace of repentance so that I may experience the times of refreshing that come with your presence.

SUGGESTIONS FOR FACILITATORS, GROUP SESSION 2

1. If there are newcomers who were not present for the first group session, introduce them now.

2. You may want to pray this prayer as a group:

   God of Abraham, Isaac, and Jacob, you have glorified your Son through his resurrection and ascension. Give us the gift of your Holy Spirit as we study the Scriptures so that we may understand your word and proclaim it with our lives. Empower us to continue the work of Jesus in the world today through the church and its ministry. Kindle in our hearts the fire of your love, and help us experience anew the grace of redemption you have brought to the world through Jesus, the Savior, Messiah, and Lord.

3. Ask one or more of the following questions:
   - What was your biggest challenge in Bible study over this past week?
   - What did you learn about yourself this week?

4. Discuss together lessons 1 through 6. Assuming that group members have read the Scripture and commentary during the week, there is no need to read it aloud. As you review each lesson, you might want to briefly summarize the Scripture passages of each lesson and ask the group what stands out most clearly from the commentary.

5. Choose one or more of the questions for reflection and discussion from each lesson to talk over as a group. You may want to ask group members which question was most challenging or helpful to them as you review each lesson.

6. Keep the discussion moving, but don't rush the discussion in order to complete more questions. Allow time for the questions that provoke the most discussion.

7. Instruct group members to complete lessons 7 through 12 on their own during the six days before the next group meeting. They should write out their own answers to the questions as preparation for next week's group discussion.

8. Conclude by praying aloud together the prayer at the end of lesson 6, or any other prayer you choose.

"Let it be known to all of you, and to all the people of Israel, that this man is standing before you in good health by the name of Jesus Christ of Nazareth." Acts 4:10

Peter and John before the Council

ACTS 4:1-22 *¹While Peter and John were speaking to the people, the priests, the captain of the temple, and the Sadducees came to them, ²much annoyed because they were teaching the people and proclaiming that in Jesus there is the resurrection of the dead. ³So they arrested them and put them in custody until the next day, for it was already evening. ⁴But many of those who heard the word believed; and they numbered about five thousand.*

⁵The next day their rulers, elders, and scribes assembled in Jerusalem, ⁶with Annas the high priest, Caiaphas, John, and Alexander, and all who were of the high-priestly family. ⁷When they had made the prisoners stand in their midst, they inquired, "By what power or by what name did you do this?" ⁸Then Peter, filled with the Holy Spirit, said to them, "Rulers of the people and elders, ⁹if we are questioned today because of a good deed done to someone who was sick and are asked how this man has been healed, ¹⁰let it be known to all of you, and to all the people of Israel, that this man is standing before you in good health by the name of Jesus Christ of Nazareth, whom you crucified, whom God raised from the dead. ¹¹This Jesus is

'the stone that was rejected by you, the builders;

36

it has become the cornerstone.'

12There is salvation in no one else, for there is no other name under heaven given among mortals by which we must be saved."

13Now when they saw the boldness of Peter and John and realized that they were uneducated and ordinary men, they were amazed and recognized them as companions of Jesus. 14When they saw the man who had been cured standing beside them, they had nothing to say in opposition. 15So they ordered them to leave the council while they discussed the matter with one another. 16They said, "What will we do with them? For it is obvious to all who live in Jerusalem that a notable sign has been done through them; we cannot deny it. 17But to keep it from spreading further among the people, let us warn them to speak no more to anyone in this name." 18So they called them and ordered them not to speak or teach at all in the name of Jesus. 19But Peter and John answered them, "Whether it is right in God's sight to listen to you rather than to God, you must judge; 20for we cannot keep from speaking about what we have seen and heard." 21After threatening them again, they let them go, finding no way to punish them because of the people, for all of them praised God for what had happened. 22For the man on whom this sign of healing had been performed was more than forty years old.

As Peter and John continue to address the people of Jerusalem about God's saving plan in Jesus and the resurrection of the dead, the religious leaders assert their authority and confront the apostles. The leaders are threatened by the growing number of those responding to the apostles, now about five thousand believers (verse 4). The episode draws a sharp contrast between the apostles and the Sanhedrin, the temple authority. Who holds the legitimate leadership over God's people? Is it the Sanhedrin, the leaders in Jerusalem who first rejected Jesus, or is it the apostles, who continue to work wonders in his name? As Acts continues, Luke demonstrates how the apostles become the true leaders of the restored Israel and rule over the twelve tribes as Jesus had predicted.

Arrested and brought to trial for the healing of the crippled man, Peter respectfully addresses his examiners. He sees this judicial inquiry as an opportunity to proclaim the name of Jesus Christ to the leaders and the people they represent. Without apology, Peter declares what he has done and by whom it was made possible. At the center of his testimony, Peter proclaims the source of the healing: "Let it be known to all of you, and to all the people of Israel, that this man is standing before you in good health by the name of Jesus Christ of Nazareth, whom you crucified, whom God raised from the dead" (verse 10). Peter, "filled with the Holy Spirit," speaks like a prophet and confronts his listeners with their own accountability. Jesus is the one whom they have crucified and whom God vindicated by raising him to life.

Peter uses the image of the discarded cornerstone to express the divine design of Jesus' rejection and vindication (verse 11). The image comes from the psalms: "The stone the builders rejected has become the cornerstone" (Ps 118:22). Jesus is that stone rejected by God's people, but made the cornerstone of God's new temple. Jesus is now the source of salvation for all humanity (verse 12). In his name God offers healing and the fullness of life to all.

The religious authorities are particularly amazed at the "boldness" of Peter and John, despite the fact that they are "uneducated and ordinary men" (verse 13). What they are unable to deny is the evidence of the power of Jesus' resurrection at work through the apostles: the healed man standing before them (verses 10, 14, 16). In their dilemma, the leaders are unable to punish the apostles, because everyone knows that "this sign of healing" was an act of God. Instead, they try to intimidate the apostles and warn them never to speak to anyone again in the name of Jesus. Will their orders prevail? We can already guess the answer.

This first indication of persecution against the apostles demonstrates that God has not called them to proclaim a gospel without sacrifice. They follow Jesus and are sent out in imitation of the one who suffered and experienced the rejection of many. These Spirit-filled apostles will not be deterred by their own fears or the threats of others. In response to the order to cease speaking in the name of Jesus, Peter and John emphatically reply, "We cannot keep from speaking about what we have seen and heard" (verse 20).

Reflection and discussion

• In what ways does the experience of the apostles in this scene parallel that of Jesus?

• Throughout Acts, Luke makes it clear that the responsibility for Jesus' crucifixion lies not only with the Jewish and Roman leaders who were involved in the historical decision to put him to death, but also with the whole human race—Jews and Gentiles—throughout time. In what sense am I guilty of the death of Jesus and in need of repentance?

• "Speaking about what we have seen and heard" is the essence of bearing witness to Jesus. How bold am I in speaking about what I have seen and heard? In what way can I bear witness to Jesus today?

• In what ways does this episode point out the limits of the power of human authorities? When is it right and just to disobey governments and institutions?

Prayer

Risen Lord, you are the rejected stone that has become the cornerstone of God's new temple. Help me overcome my fears and strengthen me to bear witness to you boldly. Let me see the signs and wonders that are happening around me, testifying to your resurrection.

"And now, Lord, look at their threats, and grant to your servants to speak your word with all boldness." Acts 4:29

The Community's Prayer for Boldness

ACTS 4:23-31 ²³*After they were released, they went to their friends and reported what the chief priests and the elders had said to them.* ²⁴*When they heard it, they raised their voices together to God and said, "Sovereign Lord, who made the heaven and the earth, the sea, and everything in them,* ²⁵*it is you who said by the Holy Spirit through our ancestor David, your servant:*

'Why did the Gentiles rage,
and the peoples imagine vain things?
²⁶*The kings of the earth took their stand,*
and the rulers have gathered together
against the Lord and against his Messiah.'

²⁷*For in this city, in fact, both Herod and Pontius Pilate, with the Gentiles and the peoples of Israel, gathered together against your holy servant Jesus, whom you anointed,* ²⁸*to do whatever your hand and your plan had predestined to take place.* ²⁹*And now, Lord, look at their threats, and grant to your servants to speak your word with all boldness,* ³⁰*while you stretch out your hand to heal, and signs and wonders are performed through the name of your holy servant Jesus."* ³¹*When they had prayed, the place in which they were gathered together was shaken; and they were all filled with the Holy Spirit and spoke the word of God with boldness.*

T he apostles are released with a warning by the religious authorities in Jerusalem, and they return to their own community of mutually supportive friends. The apostles report about their confinement and the admonition they received to cease preaching or teaching in the name of Jesus. In response, the community of believers falls to prayer, expressing their dependence on God to carry out the mission to which he has called them. They pray neither to avoid persecution nor for God's punishment on their persecutors but for strength to do God's will and to preach the message boldly in the midst of persecution.

The prayer begins with an address to God, affirming God's absolute sovereignty as the Lord and Creator (verse 24). In drawing from the opening verses of Psalm 2, the prayer affirms that this is God's word, spoken by the Holy Spirit through the voice of King David. The psalm originally addressed confidence in God and Israel's anointed king amidst the continual threats of the kings and rulers of the earth. By the time of Jesus, the psalm had come to refer to the expected Messiah and the plots against him. In applying this psalm to Jesus, the church is drawing on established Jewish tradition and Jesus' own awareness of his messianic status in God's plan. Through such Scriptures, the early Christians realize that the rejection of Jesus should not be surprising; rather, it is the expected culmination of the pattern of rejection that was a continual part of their nation's history. Opposing God's plan, whether in Israel's ancient monarchy or in the new age of the Messiah, is ultimately futile. All of the ethnic groups in Jerusalem share responsibility for the death of Jesus. The kings and rulers, represented by Herod and Pontius Pilate, as well as the Jews and Gentiles they represent, gathered together against God's Messiah (verses 26-27). Yet, through their opposition, God has been working out his saving plan.

Since many continue to resist God's plan, the church prays for the ability to respond to the opposition they face and to do God's will (verses 29-30). They ask the Lord to look upon the threats against them and to give them the ability to speak God's word with boldness. And they ask that God continue to perform signs and wonders through the name of Jesus. The preaching of the church and the visible deeds of God go hand in hand, each confirming and upholding the other. After the believers complete their prayer, God's response is demonstrated through a threefold pentecostal experience (verse 31). First, the place where they gathered is shaken, a biblical sign of God's presence among his people. Second, they are all filled with the Holy Spirit, enabling them to understand, proclaim, and witness to God's word. And third, they speak the word of God with boldness, the ability for which they had offered their prayer.

Reflection and discussion

• In preaching God's word, the community in Jerusalem walked the path of Jesus and suffered rejection. How does the opposition they faced add credibility to their preaching?

• What are some of the traits of a Spirit-led community expressed by the Jerusalem church in this episode?

• In the face of persecution, the disciples come to God in earnest prayer. How is my prayer in times of crises like or unlike this prayer?

Prayer

Sovereign Lord and Creator of all things, we trust in you, whose saving plan is the final purpose of the world. Stir up the gifts of the Holy Spirit within me, so that I may speak your word and witness in the name of Jesus, your Son.

There was not a needy person among them, for as many as owned lands or houses sold them and brought the proceeds of what was sold. Acts 4:34

Sharing Possessions in Community

ACTS 4:32–5:11 ³²*Now the whole group of those who believed were of one heart and soul, and no one claimed private ownership of any possessions, but everything they owned was held in common.* ³³*With great power the apostles gave their testimony to the resurrection of the Lord Jesus, and great grace was upon them all.* ³⁴*There was not a needy person among them, for as many as owned lands or houses sold them and brought the proceeds of what was sold.* ³⁵*They laid it at the apostles' feet, and it was distributed to each as any had need.* ³⁶*There was a Levite, a native of Cyprus, Joseph, to whom the apostles gave the name Barnabas (which means "son of encouragement").* ³⁷*He sold a field that belonged to him, then brought the money, and laid it at the apostles' feet.*

5 ¹*But a man named Ananias, with the consent of his wife Sapphira, sold a piece of property;* ²*with his wife's knowledge, he kept back some of the proceeds, and brought only a part and laid it at the apostles' feet.* ³*"Ananias," Peter asked, "why has Satan filled your heart to lie to the Holy Spirit and to keep back part of the proceeds of the land?* ⁴*While it remained unsold, did it not remain your own? And after it was sold, were not the proceeds at your disposal? How is it that*

43

you have contrived this deed in your heart? You did not lie to us but to God!" *⁵Now when Ananias heard these words, he fell down and died. And great fear seized all who heard of it. ⁶The young men came and wrapped up his body, then carried him out and buried him.*

⁷After an interval of about three hours his wife came in, not knowing what had happened. ⁸Peter said to her, "Tell me whether you and your husband sold the land for such and such a price." And she said, "Yes, that was the price." ⁹Then Peter said to her, "How is it that you have agreed together to put the Spirit of the Lord to the test? Look, the feet of those who have buried your husband are at the door, and they will carry you out." ¹⁰Immediately she fell down at his feet and died. When the young men came in they found her dead, so they carried her out and buried her beside her husband. ¹¹And great fear seized the whole church and all who heard of these things.

I n addition to great preaching and miracles, the new community of believers experiences a very personal and practical love for one another. This summary of their communal life states that they are "of one heart and soul," and their unity leads them to share their possessions so "there was not a needy person among them." Through their faith in the risen Lord, the members of the church find the source of their joy and hope in the saving power of divine love. This implies that they no longer need to cling to status and possessions for their security. Striving for genuine solidarity, they have compassion for one another, try to walk in the shoes of each other, and express a readiness to share their material resources with those in need.

The communal life of the early Christians was not a kind of top-down socialism. Their giving was totally voluntary, and sprung from an inner conviction of the worth of others and the desire to live in the power and grace of Christ's resurrection. Faith in the risen Christ is a totally transforming reality, a divine gift that, first of all, changes the minds and hearts of believers, and secondly, draws people together with a shared vision of life's meaning and purpose.

The apostles hold a central role in the early church. Their activity is expressed by two characteristics: "great power" and "great grace" (verse 33). They bear witness to the resurrection through the strength that comes from God's gracious favor. They are the overseers of the community and are at the center of its activity. Those who sold houses or property place the proceeds "at the apostles' feet" (verses 35, 37; 5:2). The good of the whole community is represented by the apostles, and they oversee the distribution of the community's resources. In all of this apostolic work, the church bears practical witness to the resurrection.

This summary of Christian life is given specific examples, both positive and negative, in the actions of Barnabas (4:36-37) and of Ananias and Sapphira (5:1-11). Barnabas, who will later be seen as the mediator between Paul and the apostles in Jerusalem, gives the proceeds of his sold property for the use of the community. His introduction here, as a positive model, heralds his heroic role throughout Acts. His name, meaning "son of encouragement," summarizes the way he will function throughout the work.

The account of Ananias and Sapphira begins with the conjunction "but," indicating that it is part of the previous section, forming a contrast to the example of Barnabas. The inclusion of this account is an honest admission that not everyone acts with virtue in the community. The couple acts deceitfully, retaining some of the proceeds of their property for themselves. They have the option of keeping the profit or disposing of only some of it. So their deceitful act is calculated and motivated by the desire to appear more generous than they truly are. They seek to gain human praise rather than to honor God. Their lying to the apostles is equivalent to lying to the Holy Spirit who lives within the church.

The hearts of this couple are motivated by Satan, indicating that the cosmic forces of evil are involved in what happens to the church. Peter, described in the previous account as "filled with the Holy Spirit," asks Ananias, "Why has Satan filled your heart to lie to the Holy Spirit?" (5:3). When Satan, rather than the Spirit of God, fills the hearts of believers, the results are the deadly sins of lies and deceit rather than honesty and faithfulness to God. Like the sin of Judas, done for money and emerging from a lying and deceitful heart, their sin results in their shocking death. The episode serves as an example to those who would "put the Spirit of the Lord to the test," seeking to deceive the one who calls them to holiness (verse 9). Since they laid money dishonestly "at the apostles' feet," they lay dead at Peter's feet (verse 10). The resulting "fear" that seizes the whole church engenders a healthy awareness that God is present in the church and can act in judgment.

Reflection and discussion

• This portrait of the early church describes a community in which its members are more concerned about what they can contribute rather than what they can receive from the church. In what ways does the individualism of our culture today undercut the development of this kind of communal life?

• Because of Jesus' resurrection, communal life among the believers led to both mission and mutual care exercised in concrete and practical ways. How might the power of Jesus' resurrection more effectively shape life within your family, religious community, or parish?

• What does it mean for people to be "of one heart and soul"? Does this describe any communities you know? What do you think made the Christian message so attractive to so many?

Prayer

Lord Jesus, give me the courage, enthusiasm, and joy of your first followers. Through your Spirit, strengthen your church to grow in number and fervor, so that all may know that the power of your resurrection is at work in us.

"We found the prison securely locked and the guards standing at the doors, but when we opened them, we found no one inside." Acts 5:23

Arrest and Imprisonment

ACTS 5:12-26 *¹²Now many signs and wonders were done among the people through the apostles. And they were all together in Solomon's Portico. ¹³None of the rest dared to join them, but the people held them in high esteem. ¹⁴Yet more than ever believers were added to the Lord, great numbers of both men and women, ¹⁵so that they even carried out the sick into the streets, and laid them on cots and mats, in order that Peter's shadow might fall on some of them as he came by. ¹⁶A great number of people would also gather from the towns around Jerusalem, bringing the sick and those tormented by unclean spirits, and they were all cured.*

¹⁷Then the high priest took action; he and all who were with him (that is, the sect of the Sadducees), being filled with jealousy, ¹⁸arrested the apostles and put them in the public prison. ¹⁹But during the night an angel of the Lord opened the prison doors, brought them out, and said, ²⁰"Go, stand in the temple and tell the people the whole message about this life." ²¹When they heard this, they entered the temple at daybreak and went on with their teaching.

When the high priest and those with him arrived, they called together the council and the whole body of the elders of Israel, and sent to the prison to have them brought. ²²But when the temple police went there, they did not find them in the prison; so they returned and reported, ²³"We found the prison securely locked and the guards standing at the doors, but when we opened them, we found no one inside." ²⁴Now when the captain of the temple and the chief priests heard these words, they were perplexed about them, wondering what might be going on. ²⁵Then someone arrived and announced, "Look, the men whom you put in prison are standing in the temple and teaching the people!" ²⁶Then the captain went with the temple police and brought them, but without violence, for they were afraid of being stoned by the people.

As the healing ministry of Jesus continues in the work of his church, the apostles bring physical and spiritual healing to people, performing "signs and wonders" on behalf of the sick and the possessed. In a culture that often linked sin with suffering and that regarded sick persons as under the power of evil spirits, the early church extends compassion and welcome to the sick. It does so in confidence that Jesus' death and resurrection has broken the power of the Evil One, that there is nothing to fear from contact with outcasts, and that the sick and suffering are God's beloved ones. The ministry of the apostles is viewed with high esteem by the people, and many men and women are added to the believing community.

Peter has followed Jesus from town to town, watching him cure the sick and heal the hopeless from despair. Now the crowds are following Peter around the streets of Jerusalem, bringing their sick on cots and mats, hoping his shadow will fall over them with a blessing (verse 15). This detail demonstrates the extent of Christ's power working through him. It is not necessarily the direct touch or even awareness of Peter that brings healing to people's lives. Their cures occur, rather, through faith in Jesus that the presence of Peter inspires within them. Peter has become so transformed through God's Spirit working within him that his closeness conveys something of the presence of Jesus to people.

The growth and success of the church is remarkable. Despite arrest and imprisonment, the preaching of the apostles cannot be contained. The greater the effort by the authorities to prevent the apostles from proclaiming the good news of Jesus, the more effective their witness becomes. The distinguished religious council of Jerusalem is embarrassed and perplexed by the information that, despite all the precautions they have taken, their prisoners are nowhere to be found. Their bewilderment is heightened when they are informed that the apostles are not only free but also are preaching again in the temple, the very crime for which they had been arrested and imprisoned.

The council is powerless to stop the spread of the word and the way of God as the apostles follow the divine mandate to continue preaching. The bafflement of the religious leaders is a strong contrast to the wondrous deeds and fearless teaching of the apostles, undaunted by threats and beatings. It is clearer now than ever that the apostles of Jesus are the true rulers of the restored Israel. Nothing will be able to stop the advance of the gospel. The opposition may be able to persecute the church, but they will never defeat the community of believers in the resurrection.

Reflection and discussion

• Believers in the risen Lord are living signs that evil has been defeated, death has been overcome by life, and sin has been overpowered by divine mercy. How can the church more effectively witness as we allow faith in the resurrection to guide us through the streets of our world?

• People still look for signs and wonders today. What do people see in my life that helps them to believe?

Prayer

Lord and Savior, you empowered Peter and the apostles to proclaim the gospel despite opposition and persecution. Release my heart from the imprisonment of fear, and make me obedient to the promptings of your Spirit.

As they left the council, they rejoiced that they were considered worthy to suffer dishonor for the sake of the name. Acts 5:41

Trial before the Council and Release

ACTS 5:27-42 *27When they had brought them, they had them stand before the council. The high priest questioned them, 28saying, "We gave you strict orders not to teach in this name, yet here you have filled Jerusalem with your teaching and you are determined to bring this man's blood on us." 29But Peter and the apostles answered, "We must obey God rather than any human authority. 30The God of our ancestors raised up Jesus, whom you had killed by hanging him on a tree. 31God exalted him at his right hand as Leader and Savior that he might give repentance to Israel and forgiveness of sins. 32And we are witnesses to these things, and so is the Holy Spirit whom God has given to those who obey him."*

33When they heard this, they were enraged and wanted to kill them. 34But a Pharisee in the council named Gamaliel, a teacher of the law, respected by all the people, stood up and ordered the men to be put outside for a short time. 35Then he said to them, "Fellow Israelites, consider carefully what you propose to do to these men. 36For some time ago Theudas rose up, claiming to be somebody, and a number of men, about four hundred, joined him; but he was killed, and all who followed him were dispersed and disappeared. 37After him Judas the Galilean rose up at the time of the census and got people to follow him; he also perished, and all who followed him were scattered. ³⁸*So in the present case, I tell you, keep away from these men and let them alone; because if this plan or this undertaking is of human origin, it will fail;* ³⁹*but if it is of God, you will not be able to overthrow them—in that case you may even be found fighting against God!"*

They were convinced by him, ⁴⁰*and when they had called in the apostles, they had them flogged. Then they ordered them not to speak in the name of Jesus, and let them go.* ⁴¹*As they left the council, they rejoiced that they were considered worthy to suffer dishonor for the sake of the name.* ⁴²*And every day in the temple and at home they did not cease to teach and proclaim Jesus as the Messiah.*

The narrative continues to demonstrate how the gospel cannot be contained. The greater the efforts to suppress God's word with arrest and threats, the more effective the witness of the apostles becomes as they teach in the name of Jesus. The impulsive abruptness that characterized Peter during the ministry of Jesus has become courageous boldness through the transformation that faith offers. Willing now to suffer and die for the sake of the gospel, his life illustrates the power of forgiveness and the transformation offered through the risen Christ. Called in before the highest authorities of Jerusalem, Peter and the apostles refuse to obey their order to be silent about Jesus. Ordered to cease preaching, Peter defiantly responds, "We must obey God rather than any human authority" (verse 29). Standing before them more as their judge than their victim, Peter the fisherman powerfully proclaims the salvation given by Jesus Christ.

The experience of faith in the Lord implies a vocation to evangelize, to pass on the good news to others. So, the apostles make it plain to the authorities who persecute them that they have no other option than to place their divine calling before all other human commands and prohibitions. The persecution of the church in Jerusalem leads to the expansion of Christianity into the regions around the city. This same pattern continues for the church throughout history. The more the church is silenced, oppressed, and persecuted, the more it grows and the stronger it becomes.

As Acts demonstrates throughout, the gospel cannot be contained, because the witness of believers is joined with that of the Spirit. As the apostles declare,

"We are witnesses to these things, and so is the Holy Spirit whom God has given to those who obey him" (verse 32). The Spirit transforms those who follow Jesus: their way of life, their outlook on the future, their relationship with one another, and their priorities. The Holy Spirit who fills their lives is the witness who confirms the human witnesses and shows that their work is the work of God.

In response to the rage of the council and the desire of the religious leaders to put the apostles to death, a voice of wise reason steps in. Gamaliel is a leading rabbi of the city, a member of the Sanhedrin, and, as we will learn later, a former teacher of Paul. After ordering that the apostles be put out of the room so that he can address the council in private, Gamaliel warns the religious leaders to "consider carefully" what they are about to do to the apostles (verse 35). A short lesson in recent history offers two examples of popular movements that quickly dispersed and faded away after the death of their founders. Gamaliel's advice, then, is to simply keep away from the apostles and leave them alone. His point is this: "If this plan or this undertaking is of human origin, it will fail" (verse 38).

Then Gamaliel presents another option: "But if it is of God, you will not be able to overthrow them—in that case you may even be found fighting against God!" (verse 39). This final comment proves to be more than practical wisdom. It is a prophetic forecast of Christianity through every age of persecution. The leaders find Gamaliel's advice persuasive, but before releasing the apostles, they have them flogged and warn them again not to speak in the name of Jesus. For their part, the apostles do what they said they would, continuing to teach openly and proclaiming Jesus as the Messiah, rejoicing that they were counted worthy to suffer dishonor in witness to his name.

Reflection and discussion

• Peter was transformed from a cowardly denier of Jesus at his passion to a courageous witness to his resurrection, willing to suffer and die for him. What does Peter teach me about being a disciple and serving his church?

• Why is it impossible to silence or suppress the good news of Jesus Christ? Why do attempts to contain the gospel usually have the opposite effects?

• What is the difference between the advice of Gamaliel and the emotional response of the other religious leaders? What is the value of Gamaliel's wait-and-see approach for discerning the will of God?

• How would I feel if I were arrested and jailed for my beliefs? How does Peter's response offer me courage and inspiration?

Prayer

Lord Jesus, I know that obedience to God must surpass my submission to any human authority. Teach me to follow the example of your apostles as they joyfully suffered dishonor for the sake of your name. Make me eager to be your witness in the world.

"Select from among yourselves seven men of good standing, full of the Spirit and of wisdom, whom we may appoint to this task, while we, for our part, will devote ourselves to prayer and to serving the word." Acts 6:3-4

Seven Chosen to Serve

ACTS 6:1-7 *¹Now during those days, when the disciples were increasing in number, the Hellenists complained against the Hebrews because their widows were being neglected in the daily distribution of food. ²And the twelve called together the whole community of the disciples and said, "It is not right that we should neglect the word of God in order to wait on tables. ³Therefore, friends, select from among yourselves seven men of good standing, full of the Spirit and of wisdom, whom we may appoint to this task, ⁴while we, for our part, will devote ourselves to prayer and to serving the word." ⁵What they said pleased the whole community, and they chose Stephen, a man full of faith and the Holy Spirit, together with Philip, Prochorus, Nicanor, Timon, Parmenas, and Nicolaus, a proselyte of Antioch. ⁶They had these men stand before the apostles, who prayed and laid their hands on them.*

⁷The word of God continued to spread; the number of the disciples increased greatly in Jerusalem, and a great many of the priests became obedient to the faith.

A cts offers a realistic account of both the wonders and the struggles of the early church. In addition to being a learning, loving, worshiping, and evangelizing community, the church also experiences both internal and external difficulties, especially as it continues to grow. We might expect this community of faith, living in the light of the resurrection and blessed with the Holy Spirit, to be free from rivalries and prejudices. Yet, the tensions grow, and Acts shows us how the community deals with these challenges and finds resolutions that serve as models for the church in every age.

Among the Jewish disciples of Jesus, there were Hellenists, who spoke Greek and favored greater assimilation of the Jewish culture with the others, and there were Hebrews, who favored sharper separation and national identity in language and culture. Consciousness of this distinction leads to suspicions of unfair discrimination, a situation that every multicultural community experiences in many forms. In this text, Hellenists complain that their widows are being neglected by the Hebrews in the daily distribution of food and clothing for those in need.

The way the church solves this difficulty is an example for resolving similar challenges in the church today. The Twelve act collegially, discerning together and gathering the community to outline the problem. Following the principle of subsidiarity, allowing the task to be performed at the lowest appropriate level, they request that the Hellenist community choose seven men to serve them in the daily task of distributing goods. These are to be chosen because of their evident goodness and integrity, "filled with the Spirit and wisdom." By appointing these men to service, through formal prayer and the laying on of hands, the apostles are able to continue their task of serving the whole community by leading prayer and engaging in the ministry of the word.

The narrative of the next three chapters is devoted to two of these men, Stephen and Philip. Though their work is described as assisting in the daily distribution and waiting at tables, at least these two, as we will see, continue the work of the apostles. They are filled with the Holy Spirit, they preach the word of God, and they work signs and wonders among the people. In the selection of these seven, we begin to see that there is a succession of authority from the apostles in order to minister to an ever-widening church. This transfer of spiritual authority is symbolized as the apostles "laid their hands on them" (verse 6). Although there is no indication that these seven were called "deacons," this episode points toward the later development of the three offices of *episcopos, presbyteros,* and *diakonos* (bishop, priest, and deacon).

By wisely resolving this internal difficulty, the unity of the church was restored. Because the community reached inwardly to resolve the crisis, its outreach flourished. In a summary verse, Luke describes the church's growth in three ways (verse 7). First, God's word spread, with the word directing its own growth like seeds producing a harvest. Second, the number of disciples increased, with God causing the expansion. And third, even many Jewish priests became obedient to the faith, another way of describing belief. Having summarized the state of the church in Jerusalem, Luke turns his attention to the expansion of the word outside Jerusalem and to the persecution that drives that spread.

Reflection and discussion

• Diversity in membership brings tensions that can either push a community positively forward or pull it negatively apart. What are some of the tensions involved in a multicultural church? How does the church today benefit from its diversity?

• The apostles realized that they could not and should not do everything in the church, but there are some tasks that they must not neglect. What can the church learn from this example of good leadership and good stewardship?

Prayer

Lord Jesus, you desire your church to be one, holy, catholic, and apostolic. Help us to heal the conflicts that arise from our diversity, and lift us up toward that greater unity which you share with the Father through the Holy Spirit.

SUGGESTIONS FOR FACILITATORS, GROUP SESSION 3

1. Welcome group members and ask if there are any announcements anyone would like to make.

2. You may want to pray this prayer as a group:

Sovereign Lord and Creator of all things, you desire the growth of your church through the proclamation of your word and the witness of believers to the resurrection of Jesus. Stir within us our baptismal fire and give us the joy, courage, and obedience of the early believers so that all will see the power of Christ's resurrection at work within us. Give us your guidance amidst the conflicts and divisions from within the church and opposition and persecution from outside the church. May we honor your call to be a church that is one, holy, catholic, and apostolic.

3. Ask one or more of the following questions:
   • Which image from lessons 7–12 stands out most memorably to you?
   • What is the most important thing you learned through your study this week?

4. Discuss lessons 7 through 12. Choose one or more of the questions for reflection and discussion from each lesson to discuss as a group. You may want to ask group members which question was most challenging or helpful to them as you review each lesson.

5. Remember that there are no definitive answers for these discussion questions. The insights of group members will add to the understanding of all. None of these questions require an expert.

6. After talking about each lesson, instruct group members to complete lessons 13 through 18 on their own during the six days before the next group meeting. They should write out their own answers to the questions as preparation for next week's group discussion.

7. Ask the group if anyone is having any particular problems with the Bible study during the week. You may want to share advice and encouragement within the group.

8. Conclude by praying aloud together the prayer at the end of one of the lessons discussed. You may add to the prayer based on the sharing that has occurred in the group.

They stirred up the people as well as the elders and the scribes; then they suddenly confronted him, seized him, and brought him before the council. Acts 6:12

The Arrest of Stephen

ACTS 6:8-15 *⁸Stephen, full of grace and power, did great wonders and signs among the people. ⁹Then some of those who belonged to the synagogue of the Freedmen (as it was called), Cyrenians, Alexandrians, and others of those from Cilicia and Asia, stood up and argued with Stephen. ¹⁰But they could not withstand the wisdom and the Spirit with which he spoke. ¹¹Then they secretly instigated some men to say, "We have heard him speak blasphemous words against Moses and God." ¹²They stirred up the people as well as the elders and the scribes; then they suddenly confronted him, seized him, and brought him before the council. ¹³They set up false witnesses who said, "This man never stops saying things against this holy place and the law; ¹⁴for we have heard him say that this Jesus of Nazareth will destroy this place and will change the customs that Moses handed on to us." ¹⁵And all who sat in the council looked intently at him, and they saw that his face was like the face of an angel.*

The account of Stephen is narrated in three parts: his arrest, speech, and martyrdom. This first part summarizes his ministry, which leads to the opposition against him. It seems that Stephen and the other seven Hellenists did much more than "wait at tables." Stephen did "great won-

58

ders and signs" and spoke with "wisdom and the Spirit," a ministry of both word and deed that appears to parallel to some extent that of the twelve apostles. He is described as "full of grace and power"; that is, he works through the enabling power of God's grace, equipped by God for what God has called him to do.

As a Hellenist, a Jew instilled with Greek language and culture, Stephen naturally ministered among the Greek-speaking Jewish Christians. As the twelve apostles served mostly the Hebrews, those Jews who spoke Aramaic and read the Scriptures in Hebrew, the seven coworkers served the Hellenists. The Holy Spirit provided workers equipped for the unique needs of the various ethnic wings of the church.

The opposition to Stephen arose from the Greek-speaking Jews, particularly from the synagogue of the Freedmen, the gathering of Jews of several different nationalities for study and prayer (verse 9). These Hellenistic Jews were strongly in support of Jewish traditions and practices, having left the lands of their birth to come to Israel, follow the Torah, and be near the temple. It seems that Stephen was presenting to them a wider interpretation of Moses, the Torah, and worship in the temple in light of the saving work of Jesus the Messiah. Threatened by Stephen's teaching but unable to match his wise eloquence, they persuaded others to testify falsely against Stephen and his message. They managed to stir up many of the established religious leaders in Jerusalem and got Stephen arrested and presented to the Sanhedrin for judgment.

The charges brought before the council blame Stephen for speaking blasphemy, that is, words of insult against Moses and God (verse 11). They charge him with opposing the temple and the law, saying that Jesus would destroy the temple and change the traditions given to them by Moses. Clearly these charges misrepresent the actual teachings of Jesus about the law and his prophecy about the temple. Stephen may have stated, like Jesus and the prophets of Israel before him, that the temple is destined for God's judgment, but to say that Jesus would destroy the temple is undoubtedly false. Stephen and the apostles argue that the church is not against the law of Israel but represents a fulfillment and completion of it.

The description of Stephen's face as "like the face of an angel" suggests that Stephen has the appearance of one whose communion with God is such that he reflects a bit of God's glory. This depiction resembles that of Moses, whose face is described as shining because he had been in the presence of God (Exod 34:29-35). This characterization of Stephen is also Luke's way of stating that Stephen is inspired by God and innocent of any wrongdoing.

The arrest and trial of Stephen imitates the passion of Jesus. As with Jesus, his religious opponents stir up the people, arrest him, and bring him before the Sanhedrin. Stephen, like Jesus, is accused by false witnesses, is charged with blasphemy, and is said to be speaking against the temple. In Stephen, as in the apostles, the ministry of Jesus—including preaching, healing, and suffering—continues.

Reflection and discussion

• What seems to be the character of Stephen, according to his description in this passage?

• Who might be the counterparts of the Hebrews and the Hellenists in the church today? How does the Holy Spirit continue to equip ministers to serve the unique needs of each group?

Prayer

Lord Jesus, you called Stephen to serve your church, filled him with your grace, and gave him wisdom and power through your Holy Spirit. Continue to raise up ministers in your church to preach, heal, and suffer in imitation of you.

"The God of glory appeared to our ancestor Abraham when he was in Mesopotamia, before he lived in Haran, and said to him, 'Leave your country and your relatives and go to the land that I will show you.'" Acts 7:2-3

God's Promises to Israel's Ancestors

ACTS 7:1-34 *¹Then the high priest asked him, "Are these things so?" ²And Stephen replied:*

"Brothers and fathers, listen to me. The God of glory appeared to our ancestor Abraham when he was in Mesopotamia, before he lived in Haran, ³and said to him, 'Leave your country and your relatives and go to the land that I will show you.' ⁴Then he left the country of the Chaldeans and settled in Haran. After his father died, God had him move from there to this country in which you are now living. ⁵He did not give him any of it as a heritage, not even a foot's length, but promised to give it to him as his possession and to his descendants after him, even though he had no child. ⁶And God spoke in these terms, that his descendants would be resident aliens in a country belonging to others, who would enslave them and mistreat them during four hundred years. ⁷'But I will judge the nation that they serve,' said God, 'and after that they shall come out and worship me in this place.' ⁸Then he gave him the covenant of circumcision. And so Abraham became the father of Isaac and circumcised him on the eighth day; and Isaac became the father of Jacob, and Jacob of the twelve patriarchs.

⁹"The patriarchs, jealous of Joseph, sold him into Egypt; but God was with him, [10]and rescued him from all his afflictions, and enabled him to win favor and to show wisdom when he stood before Pharaoh, king of Egypt, who appointed him ruler over Egypt and over all his household. [11]Now there came a famine throughout Egypt and Canaan, and great suffering, and our ancestors could find no food. [12]But when Jacob heard that there was grain in Egypt, he sent our ancestors there on their first visit. [13]On the second visit Joseph made himself known to his brothers, and Joseph's family became known to Pharaoh. [14]Then Joseph sent and invited his father Jacob and all his relatives to come to him, seventy-five in all; [15]so Jacob went down to Egypt. He himself died there as well as our ancestors, [16]and their bodies were brought back to Shechem and laid in the tomb that Abraham had bought for a sum of silver from the sons of Hamor in Shechem.

[17]"But as the time drew near for the fulfillment of the promise that God had made to Abraham, our people in Egypt increased and multiplied [18]until another king who had not known Joseph ruled over Egypt. [19]He dealt craftily with our race and forced our ancestors to abandon their infants so that they would die. [20]At this time Moses was born, and he was beautiful before God. For three months he was brought up in his father's house; [21]and when he was abandoned, Pharaoh's daughter adopted him and brought him up as her own son. [22]So Moses was instructed in all the wisdom of the Egyptians and was powerful in his words and deeds.

[23]"When he was forty years old, it came into his heart to visit his relatives, the Israelites. [24]When he saw one of them being wronged, he defended the oppressed man and avenged him by striking down the Egyptian. [25]He supposed that his kinsfolk would understand that God through him was rescuing them, but they did not understand. [26]The next day he came to some of them as they were quarreling and tried to reconcile them, saying, 'Men, you are brothers; why do you wrong each other?' [27]But the man who was wronging his neighbor pushed Moses aside, saying, 'Who made you a ruler and a judge over us? [28]Do you want to kill me as you killed the Egyptian yesterday?' [29]When he heard this, Moses fled and became a resident alien in the land of Midian. There he became the father of two sons.

[30]"Now when forty years had passed, an angel appeared to him in the wilderness of Mount Sinai, in the flame of a burning bush. [31]When Moses saw it, he was amazed at the sight; and as he approached to look, there came the voice of the Lord: [32]'I am the God of your ancestors, the God of Abraham, Isaac, and

Jacob.' Moses began to tremble and did not dare to look. ³³Then the Lord said to him, 'Take off the sandals from your feet, for the place where you are standing is holy ground. ³⁴I have surely seen the mistreatment of my people who are in Egypt and have heard their groaning, and I have come down to rescue them. Come now, I will send you to Egypt.'"

Stephen's speech is introduced by a single question of the high priest, asking whether the charges that he has been speaking blasphemous words against Moses and God are true. The response of Stephen is a remarkable overview of Israel's beginnings and the longest speech in Acts. Stephen's opponents have brought false charges and witnesses against him in order to get him to stop preaching. But Stephen uses the occasion as an opportunity to speak about why Israel is in such need of God's saving work in Jesus Christ. He convincingly uses the ancient Scriptures, which he shares with his opponents, presenting himself as faithful to Israel and highlighting the promises God made to their ancestors, Abraham, Joseph, and Moses.

Stephen addresses the members of the council as "brothers and fathers," stressing the faith and tradition he shares with them. By speaking of "the God of glory," he shows great respect for the one he is accused of blaspheming. Divine glory is God's own self-manifestation, associated with creation, covenant, Torah, the tabernacle, and the temple. God initiated his work with Israel when God appeared to Abraham, calling him to leave his own land and travel to a land God would give to his descendants. The saga continues through Isaac, Jacob, and the twelve patriarchs.

Joseph was sold into slavery because of the jealousy of his eleven brothers, but God protected him and gave him favor with Pharaoh, who appointed him ruler over Egypt. Even in the days of its patriarchs, Israel failed to recognize the one chosen by God, but God was with the one whom the others rejected. When famine hit and Jacob sends his sons to Egypt in search for food, Joseph gives them grain and eventually reveals himself to them. God has strategically placed Joseph in a position to save his people, despite his brothers' earlier rejection of him.

The saga of Moses begins over four centuries later "as the time drew near for the fulfillment of the promise that God had made to Abraham" (verse 17). Rescued in his infancy, Moses was placed by God in a position to save his people from their oppression. God protected and prepared Moses, but again, God's people failed to recognize their deliverer and rejected him (verses 25-27). Yet, God revealed himself to Moses at Mount Sinai in the flame of a burning bush. Identifying himself as the God of Abraham, Isaac, and Jacob, God called and prepared Moses to free his people from slavery. He would be another rejected instrument whom God uses to deliver his people in fulfillment of his promises to them.

Reflection and discussion

• In what ways does Stephen demonstrate that Israel's heroic ancestors were chosen and empowered by God yet rejected by their own people?

• What does Stephen's speech indicate about the importance of the Old Testament for the early Christians? Why is it important for the church today?

• Why does Stephen spend so much of his speech on Moses? What are some of the parallels he makes between Moses and Jesus?

Prayer

God of our ancestors, you raised up men and women in every age to fulfill your promises and to deliver your people from oppression. May we recognize your salvation among us and respond with confident trust in you.

"This is the Moses who said to the Israelites, 'God will raise up a prophet for you from your own people as he raised me up.'" Acts 7:37

God's Promises to Moses

ACTS 7:35-53 *[35]"It was this Moses whom they rejected when they said, 'Who made you a ruler and a judge?' and whom God now sent as both ruler and liberator through the angel who appeared to him in the bush. [36]He led them out, having performed wonders and signs in Egypt, at the Red Sea, and in the wilderness for forty years. [37]This is the Moses who said to the Israelites, 'God will raise up a prophet for you from your own people as he raised me up.' [38]He is the one who was in the congregation in the wilderness with the angel who spoke to him at Mount Sinai, and with our ancestors; and he received living oracles to give to us. [39]Our ancestors were unwilling to obey him; instead, they pushed him aside, and in their hearts they turned back to Egypt, [40]saying to Aaron, 'Make gods for us who will lead the way for us; as for this Moses who led us out from the land of Egypt, we do not know what has happened to him.' [41]At that time they made a calf, offered a sacrifice to the idol, and reveled in the works of their hands. [42]But God turned away from them and handed them over to worship the host of heaven, as it is written in the book of the prophets:*

'Did you offer to me slain victims and sacrifices
for forty years in the wilderness, O house of Israel?
[43]No; you took along the tent of Moloch,
and the star of your god Rephan,
the images that you made to worship;

so I will remove you beyond Babylon.'

[44] "Our ancestors had the tent of testimony in the wilderness, as God directed when he spoke to Moses, ordering him to make it according to the pattern he had seen. [45] Our ancestors in turn brought it in with Joshua when they dispossessed the nations that God drove out before our ancestors. And it was there until the time of David, [46] who found favor with God and asked that he might find a dwelling place for the house of Jacob. [47] But it was Solomon who built a house for him. [48] Yet the Most High does not dwell in houses made with human hands; as the prophet says,

[49] 'Heaven is my throne,
   and the earth is my footstool.
What kind of house will you build for me, says the Lord,
   or what is the place of my rest?
[50] Did not my hand make all these things?'

[51] "You stiff-necked people, uncircumcised in heart and ears, you are forever opposing the Holy Spirit, just as your ancestors used to do. [52] Which of the prophets did your ancestors not persecute? They killed those who foretold the coming of the Righteous One, and now you have become his betrayers and murderers. [53] You are the ones that received the law as ordained by angels, and yet you have not kept it."

A t this point in Stephen's speech, he leaves his narrative style and begins to make statements about Moses. He is the one who was rejected by his own people, but whom God sent as "both ruler and liberator" of them. He is the one who worked signs and wonders among the Israelites during their forty-year experience of the exodus, and the one to whom God spoke at Mount Sinai and gave him oracles for the people. Still, the Israelites refused to follow him, and they rebelled against him. They created an idol, offered sacrifices to it, and "reveled in the works of their hands" (verse 41). The quotation from the prophecies of Amos shows how the prophet rebuked the Israelites of his own time by reminding them of the earlier unfaithfulness of their ancestors in the wilderness (verses 42-43). The Israelites worship the things of creation rather than the Creator and demonstrate a recurring pattern of infidelity to the covenant and rejection of those sent by God.

The parallels Stephen draws between Moses and Jesus become increasingly obvious. Jesus is the one like Moses whom God said he would raise up from among his people. Like Moses, Jesus was sent by God as his people's deliverer yet was rejected by them. The idolatry and disobedience of Israel in their wilderness period under Moses formed a pattern that continued through the period of the prophets and into the time of Jesus.

After focusing on Moses and demonstrating how God's people have rejected the ones sent to them by God, Stephen now focuses on the tent of testimony and the temple in order to show how Israel rejected its proper worship of God (verses 44-47). The tent, which housed the ark of the covenant during Israel's wilderness period, was made according to the directions God gave to Moses. This tabernacle of the ark was brought into the land with Joshua and remained through the time of David until Solomon built the temple in Jerusalem.

Yet Stephen states that God's people must understand the limitations of this magnificent "house" for God: "The Most High does not dwell in houses made by human hands" (verse 48). Stephen is not criticizing the temple as a divinely ordained institution, just as he demonstrates great respect for Moses and the law. He is simply saying that the temple cannot contain God's presence. God's title as Most High emphasizes the divine sovereignty. The quotation from Isaiah stresses God's transcendence: the whole earth is but a footstool for God's heavenly throne (verse 49). Stephen is offering a prophetic critique of Israel's distorted view of the temple. A dwelling place made by human hands cannot be the only place God dwells.

The final section of Stephen's speech contains his climactic application of his survey of Israel's history. Because Israel's leaders have been obstinate and both their heart and ears have been unresponsive to the covenant, they have opposed the work of God as manifested by the Holy Spirit (verses 51-53). Stephen shifts from his continual reference to "our ancestors" throughout his speech to "your ancestors," separating himself from Israel's unresponsiveness. Just as they persecuted the prophets, they have now betrayed and killed the Righteous One himself. The people who have been most privileged by God, who received the Torah through God's angels, have broken God's law and his covenant and have rejected the saving gospel brought to them.

Reflection and discussion

• Why does Stephen offer the Sanhedrin this lesson in their own history? What accounts for their totally different responses to Jesus?

• How do people sometimes try to put "God in a box," trying to contain his presence and control his work? In what ways could Stephen's accusations be made against me?

• How do my insights change when I read the Old Testament in light of the Risen Christ? In what sense do the writings of our ancestors center on the coming of Jesus?

Prayer

God of our Israelite ancestors, help me to trust in your promises and know that your word is faithful. May I place my life in the midst of the great company of apostles and prophets who came before me.

Then they dragged him out of the city and began to stone him; and the witnesses laid their coats at the feet of a young man named Saul. Acts 7:58

Martyrdom of Stephen and Persecution of the Church

ACTS 7:54–8:3 *⁵⁴When they heard these things, they became enraged and ground their teeth at Stephen. ⁵⁵But filled with the Holy Spirit, he gazed into heaven and saw the glory of God and Jesus standing at the right hand of God. ⁵⁶"Look," he said, "I see the heavens opened and the Son of Man standing at the right hand of God!" ⁵⁷But they covered their ears, and with a loud shout all rushed together against him. ⁵⁸Then they dragged him out of the city and began to stone him; and the witnesses laid their coats at the feet of a young man named Saul. ⁵⁹While they were stoning Stephen, he prayed, "Lord Jesus, receive my spirit." ⁶⁰Then he knelt down and cried out in a loud voice, "Lord, do not hold this sin against them." When he had said this, he died.*

8 ¹And Saul approved of their killing him.

That day a severe persecution began against the church in Jerusalem, and all except the apostles were scattered throughout the countryside of Judea and Samaria. ²Devout men buried Stephen and made loud lamentation over him. ³But Saul was ravaging the church by entering house after house; dragging off both men and women, he committed them to prison.

The narrative of Stephen forms an important link between the gospel accounts of Jesus and the life of the early church. In recounting the entire witness of Stephen, the author demonstrates how he is both a follower and an imitator of Jesus. Like Jesus, Stephen is accused of blasphemy, and false witnesses testify against him; like Jesus, he is condemned to death and taken outside the city to be executed; like Jesus, he prays for forgiveness for his slayers; and, as Jesus delivered over his spirit to the Father, so Stephen in his final moments commits his spirit to Jesus. The parallels are made explicit in order to make the point that disciples are called to follow in the footsteps of Jesus as his witnesses in the world. As an imitator of Jesus, Stephen forms a particular example of the way the ministry of Jesus is reflected and continued in his church.

Stephen is known as the first martyr of the church because he died as the consequence of his bold profession of Christian faith. He faced his death, in imitation of Jesus, with courage and compassion. The word "martyr" derives from the Greek word for witness. Stephen gave witness to the Lord's death and resurrection in a supreme manner by giving his life to the end. He is the first in a long and glorious line of martyrs in the church, a heavenly assembly whose numbers continue to grow today.

At the moment of his death, Stephen's faith enables him to see beyond the horrible circumstances of his death to experience a vision demonstrating his intimate relationship with the Trinity. Stephen is "filled with the Holy Spirit," and he sees "the glory of God and Jesus standing at the right hand of God." Stephen's murderers, by contrast, cover their ears so that they will not hear the whispers of love emanating from God and radiating through Stephen. As disciples today, we must be able to see beyond the historical circumstances of the church in the world in order to understand how the Holy Spirit fills the church and unites believers with the Father and with Jesus at his side in glory.

The death of Stephen marks a turning point in Luke's narrative of the early church. His stoning ends on an ominous note: "The witnesses laid their coats at the feet of a young man named Saul" (verse 58), who also approved of their killing Stephen (8:1). Here Luke notes Saul's role in the increasing persecution of Christian believers and also introduces the hero of the second half of Acts. As Stephen is buried and his death lamented, Saul begins to arrest and imprison believers (8:2-3). As the followers of Jesus scatter from Jerusalem to the surrounding areas of Judea and Samaria because of the persecution, they also begin to spread the gospel to those regions and beyond. This transition also prepares for the remarkable transformation of Saul the persecutor into Paul the apostle.

Reflection and discussion

• What is the significance of the parallelism between Luke's accounts of Jesus' death and Stephen's martyrdom? What does this text teach me about Christian death?

• Why are the martyrs of the church such powerful witnesses to the gospel? Who is a martyr you admire from the church's past centuries? Who would you consider to be a modern-day martyr?

• Luke's first mention of Saul/Paul notes that he witnessed the stoning of Stephen and implies that it must have made an impact on him. How could witnessing Stephen's death prepare Saul's heart for repentance and faith?

Prayer

Son of Man, you live in glory at the side of the Father in heaven. Fill me with your Holy Spirit so that I can experience divine life and overcome the world's hostility to you. Give me the grace to be a fervent witness to your resurrection.

Now when the apostles at Jerusalem heard that Samaria had accepted the word of God, they sent Peter and John to them. The two went down and prayed for them that they might receive the Holy Spirit. Acts 8:14-15

Philip's Witness in Samaria

ACTS 8:4-25 *⁴Now those who were scattered went from place to place, proclaiming the word. ⁵Philip went down to the city of Samaria and proclaimed the Messiah to them. ⁶The crowds with one accord listened eagerly to what was said by Philip, hearing and seeing the signs that he did, ⁷for unclean spirits, crying with loud shrieks, came out of many who were possessed; and many others who were paralyzed or lame were cured. ⁸So there was great joy in that city.*

⁹Now a certain man named Simon had previously practiced magic in the city and amazed the people of Samaria, saying that he was someone great. ¹⁰All of them, from the least to the greatest, listened to him eagerly, saying, "This man is the power of God that is called Great." ¹¹And they listened eagerly to him because for a long time he had amazed them with his magic. ¹²But when they believed Philip, who was proclaiming the good news about the kingdom of God and the name of Jesus Christ, they were baptized, both men and women. ¹³Even Simon himself believed. After being baptized, he stayed constantly with Philip and was amazed when he saw the signs and great miracles that took place.

¹⁴Now when the apostles at Jerusalem heard that Samaria had accepted the word of God, they sent Peter and John to them. ¹⁵The two went down and prayed for them that they might receive the Holy Spirit ¹⁶(for as yet the Spirit had not come upon any of them; they had only been baptized in the name of the Lord

Jesus). ¹⁷Then Peter and John laid their hands on them, and they received the Holy Spirit. ¹⁸Now when Simon saw that the Spirit was given through the laying on of the apostles' hands, he offered them money, ¹⁹saying, "Give me also this power so that anyone on whom I lay my hands may receive the Holy Spirit." ²⁰But Peter said to him, "May your silver perish with you, because you thought you could obtain God's gift with money! ²¹You have no part or share in this, for your heart is not right before God. ²²Repent therefore of this wickedness of yours, and pray to the Lord that, if possible, the intent of your heart may be forgiven you. ²³For I see that you are in the gall of bitterness and the chains of wickedness." ²⁴Simon answered, "Pray for me to the Lord, that nothing of what you have said may happen to me."

²⁵Now after Peter and John had testified and spoken the word of the Lord, they returned to Jerusalem, proclaiming the good news to many villages of the Samaritans.

Ironically, the persecution of the church in Jerusalem, which was initiated with the martyrdom of Stephen, has the opposite effect of its intention. The dispersion of the church beyond Jerusalem leads to a widened preaching of the word (verse 4). This scattering begins the second stage of evangelization narrated in Acts—the witness in Judea and Samaria (1:8). As the ministry of Philip begins to show, the scattered seed of God's word bears an increasingly wide harvest for the gospel.

In going to the Samaritans, Philip is reaching out to the margins. The Samaritans were held in contempt by the Jews in Jerusalem because they were considered to be unfaithful to the covenant and of mixed ancestry. Philip's intrepid venture continues a mission begun by Jesus, when he encountered the Samaritan woman at a well and she brought her townspeople to believe in him as Savior of the world. Through Philip's ministry, the Samaritans at last hear the full gospel of Jesus' resurrection. The church's understanding of the boundaries of God's people is changing rapidly. No one would ever have thought that the despised Samaritans would become disciples of the Jewish Messiah. But guided by the Spirit, Philip invites them into full participation in the restored people of God. As a result of Philip's proclamation of the gospel in word and deed, many come to believe in the good news of God's kingdom and are baptized (verse 12).

In order to demonstrate the continuity between the work of the first missionaries and the ministry of the apostles in Jerusalem, Peter and John are sent to confirm the faith and baptisms of these new Christians. The apostles' prayers and the laying on of hands provide a physical and sacramental link between the apostles and the work of the expanding church (verse 17). They embrace the Samaritans as brothers and sisters in the newly expanding family of God made known in the resurrection of Jesus. The Samaritans receive the Holy Spirit, and so they share with the other disciples in the joy, courage, confidence, and self-dedication which mark those anointed by the Spirit.

Among those who come to believe the good news and to be baptized is a man named Simon, who has so amazed the people of Samaria by his practice of magic that the people believed his power to be divine (verse 10). When he sees the power of the Holy Spirit communicated "through the laying on of the apostles' hands," he offers to purchase this power for himself (verse 19). But Peter rebukes him and urges him to repent, saying, "Your heart is not right before God," and "You are in the gall of bitterness and the chains of wickedness" (verses 21-23). Peter's severe admonishment demonstrates that Christianity has nothing to do with magic, that the Holy Spirit cannot be manipulated, and that divine power cannot be bought. The work of the Spirit must be received as a benevolent act and a grace from God. Although Simon's faith is not genuine and he represents powers opposed to God's kingdom, his request for prayers offers us hope that he will repent of his wickedness, trust in God's grace, and be forgiven.

Reflection and discussion

• During the growing persecution of the church in the second century, Tertullian wrote: "The blood of the martyrs is the seed of the Church." In what way does the martyrdom of Stephen show this to be true in the church in the age of the apostles? How is it true also today?

• Philip's ministry in Samaria indicates how the Holy Spirit impels the church outward, breaking down previously held boundaries. How might the church follow this same impulse of the Spirit today?

• What do Philip and Simon have in common? How are they different?

• What is the difference between miracles and magic? Why can the power of God's Spirit be neither manipulated nor purchased?

Prayer

Risen Lord, you send your disciples to continue your mission in ways they don't expect. Help me not to set limits on where you might ask me to go, what you might ask me to do, or how you might ask me to serve you.

Then Philip began to speak, and starting with this scripture, he proclaimed to him the good news about Jesus. Acts 8:35

Philip and the Ethiopian

ACTS 8:26-40 *²⁶Then an angel of the Lord said to Philip, "Get up and go toward the south to the road that goes down from Jerusalem to Gaza." (This is a wilderness road.) ²⁷So he got up and went. Now there was an Ethiopian eunuch, a court official of the Candace, queen of the Ethiopians, in charge of her entire treasury. He had come to Jerusalem to worship ²⁸and was returning home; seated in his chariot, he was reading the prophet Isaiah. ²⁹Then the Spirit said to Philip, "Go over to this chariot and join it." ³⁰So Philip ran up to it and heard him reading the prophet Isaiah. He asked, "Do you understand what you are reading?" ³¹He replied, "How can I, unless someone guides me?" And he invited Philip to get in and sit beside him. ³²Now the passage of the scripture that he was reading was this:*

"Like a sheep he was led to the slaughter,
*   and like a lamb silent before its shearer,*
*   so he does not open his mouth.*
³³In his humiliation justice was denied him.
*   Who can describe his generation?*
*   For his life is taken away from the earth."*

³⁴The eunuch asked Philip, "About whom, may I ask you, does the prophet say this, about himself or about someone else?" ³⁵Then Philip began to speak, and

starting with this scripture, he proclaimed to him the good news about Jesus.
³⁶As they were going along the road, they came to some water; and the eunuch
said, "Look, here is water! What is to prevent me from being baptized?" ³⁸He
commanded the chariot to stop, and both of them, Philip and the eunuch, went
down into the water, and Philip baptized him. ³⁹When they came up out of the
water, the Spirit of the Lord snatched Philip away; the eunuch saw him no more,
and went on his way rejoicing. ⁴⁰But Philip found himself at Azotus, and as he
was passing through the region, he proclaimed the good news to all the towns
until he came to Caesarea.

From Samaria, Philip is sent southward back into Judea, to the road
that leads southwestward from Jerusalem to Gaza. There he encounters an Ethiopian, the treasurer to the queen of Ethiopia. He is returning from Jerusalem to his home, which is south of Egypt and deeper into
Africa, a round trip lasting several months. Through this Ethiopian, the ministry of Philip brings the gospel not only into the regions of Judea but even to
a new continent.

Traveling along the wilderness road in his chariot, the Ethiopian is reading
aloud from a scroll of the prophet Isaiah. God's Spirit prompted Philip to
approach the chariot and ask the man if he comprehends what he is reading.
The Ethiopian admits that he needs a guide and invites Philip into the chariot
to lead him in a discussion about the meaning of the Isaian text (verses
30-31).

The passage with which they begin is that of Isaiah 53, commonly called the
song of the Suffering Servant. In the Judaism of the time, the rabbis discussed
how the subject of the passage could be the prophet himself, the people of
Israel personified, or a coming Messiah. When the Ethiopian asks who the
passage is speaking about, Philip makes clear to him how the passage ultimately refers to Jesus Christ. He explains how Jesus is that servant who suffered unjustly, and how his death, which seems like a tragic loss, resulted in
everything being gained. Then, using other passages of Scripture as well, he
proclaims to him the good news of salvation. As Jesus opened the meaning of
the Scriptures about himself on the road to Emmaus (Luke 24:27), so Philip
opens the Scriptures to the Ethiopian on the road to Gaza (verse 35).

The Ethiopian is a man of much power and authority, yet he is humble enough to know that he does not understand the word of God, and so he is receptive to the truth. Philip's proclamation of the good news leads the Ethiopian to faith, and when they arrive at a place of water, the believing Ethiopian requests to be baptized. Both Philip and the Ethiopian go down into the water, and Philip baptizes the new convert. When they come out of the water, Philip's work is complete, and God's Spirit takes hold of him and brings him to new missions along the coast.

The evangelizing mission of the church is reaching out beyond Jerusalem, to Samaria and Judea, and increasingly to the ends of the earth. Philip's mission is clearly divinely led, prodded by the Holy Spirit. In obedience to God, Philip has been led to Samaria, of all places, and now along a desert road to encounter, of all people, an Ethiopian. Responsive to the Spirit, Philip and other evangelizers like him find themselves in the oddest of situations with the most surprising sorts of people. The text presents the stages of baptismal preparation in the early church: the preaching of the good news of Jesus, the interpretation of the Scriptures as preparation, the profession of faith on the part of the believer, and the solemn entry into the water of baptism.

Reflection and discussion

• Read Isaiah 53. Do I know the Old Testament well enough to answer questions posed to me like those of the Ethiopian?

• If I were Philip, how would I use Isaiah 53 to proclaim the good news about Jesus?

• What kinds of people are beyond my boundary of comfort and familiarity? How might God be inviting me to get to know and serve someone outside my comfort zone?

• The Ethiopian did not understand his reading and requested a guide. Do I take the time to understand what I am reading in the Scriptures? Am I taking advantage of opportunities to be taught the Scriptures by others?

• What evidence of both human initiative and divine work is present in this encounter? In what ways is evangelization a result of both human efforts and divine grace?

Prayer

Spirit of God, you inspired the writing of Scripture, and you give the church guides to its interpretation. Help me to take advantage of the guidance you offer me, and lead me to direct others as we listen to God's word and act on it.

SUGGESTIONS FOR FACILITATORS, GROUP SESSION 4

1. Welcome group members and ask if anyone has any questions, announcements, or requests.

2. You may want to pray this prayer as a group:

> *Father of our Lord Jesus, you have placed your church in the midst of the great company of Israelite heroes, prophets, apostles, and evangelists who have come before us. You raised up Stephen to preach, heal, and suffer in imitation of your Son. You called Philip to interpret your word and proclaim the gospel in remote places. Continue to lift up ministers in your church, and give us the grace to be witnesses to Jesus. Help us not to set limits on where you might ask us to go, what you might ask us to do, and how you might ask us to serve.*

3. Ask one or more of the following questions:
   - What is the most difficult part of this study for you?
   - What insights stand out to you from the lessons this week?

4. Discuss lessons 13 through 18. Choose one or more of the questions for reflection and discussion from each lesson to discuss as a group. You may want to ask group members which question was most challenging or helpful to them as you review each lesson.

5. Keep the discussion moving, but allow time for the questions that provoke the most discussion. Encourage the group members to use "I" language in their responses.

6. After talking over each lesson, instruct group members to complete lessons 19 through 24 on their own during the six days before the next group meeting. They should write out their own answers to the questions as preparation for next week's session.

7. Ask the group what encouragement they need for the coming week. Ask the members to pray for the needs of one another during the week.

8. Conclude by praying aloud together the prayer at the end of one of the lessons discussed. You may choose to conclude the prayer by asking members to pray aloud any requests they may have.

"Go, for he is an instrument whom I have chosen to bring my name before Gentiles and kings and before the people of Israel; I myself will show him how much he must suffer for the sake of my name." Acts 9:15-16

The Persecutor Becomes the Persecuted

ACTS 9:1-31 *¹Meanwhile Saul, still breathing threats and murder against the disciples of the Lord, went to the high priest ²and asked him for letters to the synagogues at Damascus, so that if he found any who belonged to the Way, men or women, he might bring them bound to Jerusalem. ³Now as he was going along and approaching Damascus, suddenly a light from heaven flashed around him. ⁴He fell to the ground and heard a voice saying to him, "Saul, Saul, why do you persecute me?" ⁵He asked, "Who are you, Lord?" The reply came, "I am Jesus, whom you are persecuting. ⁶But get up and enter the city, and you will be told what you are to do." ⁷The men who were traveling with him stood speechless because they heard the voice but saw no one. ⁸Saul got up from the ground, and though his eyes were open, he could see nothing; so they led him by the hand and brought him into Damascus. ⁹For three days he was without sight, and neither ate nor drank.*

¹⁰Now there was a disciple in Damascus named Ananias. The Lord said to him in a vision, "Ananias." He answered, "Here I am, Lord." ¹¹The Lord said to him, "Get up and go to the street called Straight, and at the house of Judas look for a man of Tarsus named Saul. At this moment he is praying, ¹²and he has seen

81

in a vision a man named Ananias come in and lay his hands on him so that he might regain his sight." *13But* Ananias answered, "Lord, I have heard from many about this man, how much evil he has done to your saints in Jerusalem; *14and* here he has authority from the chief priests to bind all who invoke your name." *15But* the Lord said to him, "Go, for he is an instrument whom I have chosen to bring my name before Gentiles and kings and before the people of Israel; *16I* myself will show him how much he must suffer for the sake of my name." *17So* Ananias went and entered the house. He laid his hands on Saul and said, "Brother Saul, the Lord Jesus, who appeared to you on your way here, has sent me so that you may regain your sight and be filled with the Holy Spirit." *18And* immediately something like scales fell from his eyes, and his sight was restored. Then he got up and was baptized, *19and* after taking some food, he regained his strength.

For several days he was with the disciples in Damascus, *20and* immediately he began to proclaim Jesus in the synagogues, saying, "He is the Son of God." *21All* who heard him were amazed and said, "Is not this the man who made havoc in Jerusalem among those who invoked this name? And has he not come here for the purpose of bringing them bound before the chief priests?" *22Saul* became increasingly more powerful and confounded the Jews who lived in Damascus by proving that Jesus was the Messiah.

23After some time had passed, the Jews plotted to kill him, *24but* their plot became known to Saul. They were watching the gates day and night so that they might kill him; *25but* his disciples took him by night and let him down through an opening in the wall, lowering him in a basket.

26When he had come to Jerusalem, he attempted to join the disciples; and they were all afraid of him, for they did not believe that he was a disciple. *27But* Barnabas took him, brought him to the apostles, and described for them how on the road he had seen the Lord, who had spoken to him, and how in Damascus he had spoken boldly in the name of Jesus. *28So* he went in and out among them in Jerusalem, speaking boldly in the name of the Lord. *29He* spoke and argued with the Hellenists; but they were attempting to kill him. *30When* the believers learned of it, they brought him down to Caesarea and sent him off to Tarsus.

31Meanwhile the church throughout Judea, Galilee, and Samaria had peace and was built up. Living in the fear of the Lord and in the comfort of the Holy Spirit, it increased in numbers.

T he mysterious man who was holding the garments of those who stoned Stephen and who persecuted and imprisoned many believers now takes center stage in Luke's narrative. Saul, also known as Paul, is transformed from persecutor to apostle in one of history's most remarkable conversions. The event is so important that Luke gives us three versions, once here and twice in Paul's defense speeches (22:6-21; 26:12-18), each offering some new aspect of the event's significance.

The light of Saul's divine encounter is so intense that he falls to the ground. The flashing light, the divine voice, and the double calling out of his name reminds us of God's manifestations to Moses (Exod 3:2-4). Although he does not immediately realize it, Saul is seeing the full glory of the risen Jesus. The divine voice asks Saul why he is persecuting him, pointing to Jesus' corporate solidarity with his church. Saul's conversion from persecutor of the church to its greatest evangelist expresses the ironic truth of Gamaliel's prophetic words: "If it is of God, you will not be able to overthrow them" (5:39). Saul's failure to destroy the movement and his radical transformation into its advocate is a sure sign that Jesus is the risen Lord and that the movement comes from God. Saul the persecutor, who was headed to Damascus with a letter from the high priest, is now Saul the witness, sent with a commission from Jesus Christ.

Luke describes the young church with a number of terms in this passage: it is "the disciples of the Lord" (verse 1), "the Way" (verse 2), the living presence of Jesus in the world (verse 5), "the saints" (verse 13), and "all who invoke [the name of the Lord]" (verse 14; 2:21). Into this community of believers, Saul is brought helpless and blind (verse 8). For three days he sits in darkness and fasts from food and drink in repentance, awaiting his baptism. He needs the faith of an obscure believer named Ananias and the gift of the Spirit through baptism in order to know what to do and to have the strength to do it (verses 17-19). In persecuting the church, he was persecuting Christ (verses 4-5), but now in being part of this community of believers, he belongs to Christ.

The Lord had told Ananias that Saul's calling would involve suffering: "I myself will show him how much he must suffer for the sake of my name" (verse 16). After Saul began to proclaim Jesus as Messiah and Son of God in the synagogue of Damascus, Luke recounts the first of many sufferings Saul would endure in his life. A plot arises to kill him, with the conspirators keeping careful watch over the city gates. But Saul's followers lower him down the walls in a basket one night, allowing him to escape from the city (verse 25).

When Saul comes to Jerusalem, he continues to experience suffering: he is feared by the disciples and they do not trust that he has become a disciple (verse 26). But Barnabas, the "son of encouragement" (4:36), takes Saul under his wing and introduces him to the apostles, describing Saul's conversion and his courageous preaching in Damascus (verse 27). Barnabas will be a key companion of Saul later on. Here, only someone so respected by the community as Barnabas could bring the church to lay aside its fears of Saul. But another plot arises against Saul in Jerusalem. Some Greek-speaking Jews try to take his life, but he is rescued by the believers, who bring him to coastal Caesarea and then send him off to his native Tarsus (verses 29-30).

The summary note refers to the one church in three different regions: Judea, Galilee, and Samaria (verse 31). It enjoys peace and spiritual growth because of its respectful fear of God and the comforting encouragement of the Holy Spirit. Despite the persecution it endures, the church continues to flourish and increase in number.

Reflection and discussion

• Why would Jesus have chosen a zealous enemy of the church as his instrument to evangelize the nations?

• What were some of the conflicting emotions Paul must have experienced in Damascus and Jerusalem?

• Which term used for the church in this chapter best expresses my experience? How does the example of Saul help me to understand the church in this way?

• Paul's encounter with Christ brought him from a state of zealous certainty to a condition of helpless dependence. Why is humble trust so necessary for living a life in Christ?

• How did Saul experience forgiveness both from God and from the community he sought to destroy? Why did receiving forgiveness empower him to minister more boldly and humbly?

Prayer

Lord Jesus, you appeared to Paul and transformed his life. Help me to accept suffering as a path to my growth in you. Break into my life and change my complacency to zeal, my confusion to understanding, my apathy to love.

He turned to the body and said, "Tabitha, get up."
Then she opened her eyes, and seeing Peter, she sat up. Acts 9:40

Peter Heals in the Name of Jesus Christ

ACTS 9:32-43 *32Now as Peter went here and there among all the believers, he came down also to the saints living in Lydda. 33There he found a man named Aeneas, who had been bedridden for eight years, for he was paralyzed. 34Peter said to him, "Aeneas, Jesus Christ heals you; get up and make your bed!" And immediately he got up. 35And all the residents of Lydda and Sharon saw him and turned to the Lord.*

36Now in Joppa there was a disciple whose name was Tabitha, which in Greek is Dorcas. She was devoted to good works and acts of charity. 37At that time she became ill and died. When they had washed her, they laid her in a room upstairs. 38Since Lydda was near Joppa, the disciples, who heard that Peter was there, sent two men to him with the request, "Please come to us without delay." 39So Peter got up and went with them; and when he arrived, they took him to the room upstairs. All the widows stood beside him, weeping and showing tunics and other clothing that Dorcas had made while she was with them. 40Peter put all of them outside, and then he knelt down and prayed. He turned to the body and said, "Tabitha, get up." Then she opened her eyes, and seeing Peter, she sat up. 41He gave her his hand and helped her up. Then calling the saints and widows, he showed her to be alive. 42This became known throughout Joppa, and many believed in the Lord. ^{43}*Meanwhile he stayed in Joppa for some time with a certain Simon, a tanner.*

T he narrative now returns to Peter, who is making pastoral visits to the communities of believers outside Jerusalem. The city of Lydda is about twenty-five miles west of Jerusalem within the Plain of Sharon. Joppa is another day's journey along the coast of the Mediterranean Sea. His apostolic visits are directed to communities of "the saints" which have already been formed among the Jews of the region, although these regions are populated with both Jews and Gentiles. This transition draws Peter further into the world of the Gentiles where he will soon inaugurate their evangelization.

In Lydda, Peter is introduced to Aeneas, a paralytic who had been confined to his bed for eight years. Peter tells him to arise, making it clear that Peter is the mediator of divine healing, but that the risen Jesus is the healer (verse 34). Peter's instruction, "Get up and make your bed," shows that Aeneas is restored to health and can now care for himself. With his new vitality, Aeneas becomes a witness to what Jesus can do, so that many residents of the area become believers.

At Joppa, a disciple named Tabitha, who was known for her good works and charitable giving, has become sick and died, causing deeply felt grief among the church there. Hearing that Peter is visiting nearby Lydda, emissaries are sent to bring him to Tabitha (verse 38). When Peter arrives at the upstairs room where her body lay, the widows are weeping and showing him the clothing she had made for them (verse 39).

Peter asks all to leave the room, and he kneels, beseeching God in prayer (verse 40). Peter then turns to the woman and issues the command, "Tabitha, get up." She opens her eyes, sees Peter, and sits up. Peter then offers his hand and helps her up. When Peter calls the community together and presents her alive, the word spreads and many more believe in the Lord.

Luke shows clear parallels between the healings of Jesus in the gospel and those of Peter. The healing of Aeneas is similar to Jesus' cure of the paralytic. Jesus commanded the healed man to get up, pick up his bed, and go home, a similar indication that the man was then able to care for himself (Luke 5:24). Peter's resuscitation of Tabitha echoes similar accounts in the gospel. At the raising of Jairus' daughter, Jesus cleared the room and commanded the girl to get up (Luke 8:54-55). Peter's word of command in Aramaic would have been, "Tabitha, cumi," which is only slightly different from the traditional words of Jesus to the young girl, "Talitha, cumi." These parallels are no coincidence. Peter's ministry demonstrates that Jesus is still powerfully at work in his church.

Reflection and discussion

• What are some of the similarities in these narratives of Peter at Lydda and Joppa? What does Luke indicate through these parallels?

• How do these accounts demonstrate that the source of Peter's healing power is the resurrection of Jesus? How do these scenes speak to me about the role of the risen Lord in my life?

• Why does Luke show us echoes of Jesus' miracles in these works of Peter? What is the ultimate result of Peter's healing the sick and raising the dead?

Prayer

Risen Lord, through the ministry of your church your power is at work, as the sick are restored to health and the dead are raised to life. Give me a desire to bring your healing peace and loving wholeness to people in the world today.

"Cornelius, a centurion, an upright and God-fearing man, who is well spoken of by the whole Jewish nation, was directed by a holy angel to send for you to come to his house and to hear what you have to say." Acts 10:22

Visions of Cornelius and Peter

ACTS 10:1-23 *¹In Caesarea there was a man named Cornelius, a centurion of the Italian Cohort, as it was called. ²He was a devout man who feared God with all his household; he gave alms generously to the people and prayed constantly to God. ³One afternoon at about three o'clock he had a vision in which he clearly saw an angel of God coming in and saying to him, "Cornelius." ⁴He stared at him in terror and said, "What is it, Lord?" He answered, "Your prayers and your alms have ascended as a memorial before God. ⁵Now send men to Joppa for a certain Simon who is called Peter; ⁶he is lodging with Simon, a tanner, whose house is by the seaside." ⁷When the angel who spoke to him had left, he called two of his slaves and a devout soldier from the ranks of those who served him, ⁸and after telling them everything, he sent them to Joppa.*

⁹About noon the next day, as they were on their journey and approaching the city, Peter went up on the roof to pray. ¹⁰He became hungry and wanted something to eat; and while it was being prepared, he fell into a trance. ¹¹He saw the heaven opened and something like a large sheet coming down, being lowered to the ground by its four corners. ¹²In it were all kinds of four-footed creatures and reptiles and birds of the air. ¹³Then he heard a voice saying, "Get up, Peter; kill

89

and eat." [14]*But Peter said, "By no means, Lord; for I have never eaten anything that is profane or unclean." [15]The voice said to him again, a second time, "What God has made clean, you must not call profane." [16]This happened three times, and the thing was suddenly taken up to heaven.*

[17]*Now while Peter was greatly puzzled about what to make of the vision that he had seen, suddenly the men sent by Cornelius appeared. They were asking for Simon's house and were standing by the gate. [18]They called out to ask whether Simon, who was called Peter, was staying there. [19]While Peter was still thinking about the vision, the Spirit said to him, "Look, three men are searching for you. [20]Now get up, go down, and go with them without hesitation; for I have sent them." [21]So Peter went down to the men and said, "I am the one you are looking for; what is the reason for your coming?" [22]They answered, "Cornelius, a centurion, an upright and God-fearing man, who is well spoken of by the whole Jewish nation, was directed by a holy angel to send for you to come to his house and to hear what you have to say." [23]So Peter invited them in and gave them lodging.*

The experiences that lead Peter to the house of Cornelius prepare the church for a broader understanding of itself that will open the gospel to people of all nations. The church has already overcome previous divisions between rich and poor, slave and free, male and female. Now the final barrier, the most difficult, was about to be broken. The racial, cultural, and religious wall that divided Jews and Gentiles was the supreme test of the power of God's Spirit at work among the early Christians. The reception of the Gentiles into the church will initiate the fundamental step of bringing Christianity from an ethnic religion of Jews to a truly universal faith.

The parallel visions of Cornelius and Peter are each received in the context of prayer, emphasizing that the visions and the episodes that follow are divinely directed. God is working in both men: preparing Cornelius to receive the good news of Jesus Christ and preparing Peter to offer it to him. Both are in need of a conversion. They each require a change of mind and heart if the saving plan of God for all people is to go forward.

Although Cornelius was highly regarded by the Jewish people, he was a Gentile military officer stationed in Caesarea, the seacoast city that served as the capital of the Roman forces. As such, he represented the oppressive empire that held Israel in subjugation. Yet, the angel in his vision tells him that his prayers and alms rise to God like a sacrifice offered in the temple (verse 4). God was clearly working in the life of this outsider, breaking down the barrier that for so long had been assumed to be God's will.

While the men sent by Cornelius are approaching Joppa, Peter is given a vision that reveals God's will. In the vision, Peter is shown a smorgasbord of living creatures to satisfy his hunger. Three times Peter is invited to kill and eat the animals, reptiles, and birds presented on the sheet (verse 13). The Jewish dietary prohibitions specified in Leviticus 11 distinguish between animals that may be eaten, known as "clean," and animals that may not be eaten, known as "unclean." Peter protests the command to eat, saying that he has never eaten anything profane or unclean. But, in contrast to Peter's Jewish practice, the heavenly voice insists, "What God has made clean, you must not call profane" (verse 15).

The same prohibitions that separated animals into clean and unclean also divided people from one another. Peter came to realize that his symbolic vision was not only about food laws but also about fellowship and acceptance. It expressed God's will to remove the barriers that divided Jews and Gentiles. If God is making unclean food clean, the Jewish Christians may share table fellowship with Gentiles and cross the barriers that prevented the gospel from being brought to all people.

While Peter was still puzzling over his vision, the three men sent by Cornelius arrive at his gate. Peter is urged by God's Spirit to go to them and comply with their requests. As the men explain to Peter the purpose of their mission, he begins to understand the meaning and purpose of his vision. He hosts the men overnight in preparation for their momentous journey the next day to the house of Cornelius.

Reflection and discussion

• In what sense could Peter's vision about animals that may be eaten be also about acceptance of people? How was Peter's partiality limiting God's work?

• Could it be that God's vision of who is part of his people today is broader than mine? How might my partiality limit God's work?

• When has a cultural or religious belief of mine been questioned, challenged, or altered by further evidence or experience?

• What are some of the barriers that divide people from one another? In what ways does the gospel break down these barriers?

Prayer

Lord of all nations, you have created all creatures, and you rule over all peoples. As you enabled Peter to overcome the barriers that separated him from people longing for the gospel, open my mind to your vision so that I may be an instrument of evangelization in your church.

"I truly understand that God shows no partiality, but in every nation anyone who fears him and does what is right is acceptable to him." Acts 10:34-35

Gentiles Receive the Good News

ACTS 10:23-48 *²³The next day he got up and went with them, and some of the believers from Joppa accompanied him. ²⁴The following day they came to Caesarea. Cornelius was expecting them and had called together his relatives and close friends. ²⁵On Peter's arrival Cornelius met him, and falling at his feet, worshiped him. ²⁶But Peter made him get up, saying, "Stand up; I am only a mortal." ²⁷And as he talked with him, he went in and found that many had assembled; ²⁸and he said to them, "You yourselves know that it is unlawful for a Jew to associate with or to visit a Gentile; but God has shown me that I should not call anyone profane or unclean. ²⁹So when I was sent for, I came without objection. Now may I ask why you sent for me?"*

³⁰Cornelius replied, "Four days ago at this very hour, at three o'clock, I was praying in my house when suddenly a man in dazzling clothes stood before me. ³¹He said, 'Cornelius, your prayer has been heard and your alms have been remembered before God. ³²Send therefore to Joppa and ask for Simon, who is called Peter; he is staying in the home of Simon, a tanner, by the sea.' ³³Therefore I sent for you immediately, and you have been kind enough to come. So now all of us are here in the presence of God to listen to all that the Lord has commanded you to say."

³⁴Then Peter began to speak to them: "I truly understand that God shows no partiality, [35]but in every nation anyone who fears him and does what is right is acceptable to him. [36]You know the message he sent to the people of Israel, preaching peace by Jesus Christ—he is Lord of all. [37]That message spread throughout Judea, beginning in Galilee after the baptism that John announced: [38]how God anointed Jesus of Nazareth with the Holy Spirit and with power; how he went about doing good and healing all who were oppressed by the devil, for God was with him. [39]We are witnesses to all that he did both in Judea and in Jerusalem. They put him to death by hanging him on a tree; [40]but God raised him on the third day and allowed him to appear, [41]not to all the people but to us who were chosen by God as witnesses, and who ate and drank with him after he rose from the dead. [42]He commanded us to preach to the people and to testify that he is the one ordained by God as judge of the living and the dead. [43]All the prophets testify about him that everyone who believes in him receives forgiveness of sins through his name."

[44]While Peter was still speaking, the Holy Spirit fell upon all who heard the word. [45]The circumcised believers who had come with Peter were astounded that the gift of the Holy Spirit had been poured out even on the Gentiles, [46]for they heard them speaking in tongues and extolling God. Then Peter said, [47]"Can anyone withhold the water for baptizing these people who have received the Holy Spirit just as we have?" [48]So he ordered them to be baptized in the name of Jesus Christ. Then they invited him to stay for several days.

P eter takes the first step in opening the church to the Gentiles by walking through the open door of Cornelius' house. Cornelius has prepared for Peter's arrival by inviting his close friends and relatives to hear him. At Peter's arrival, Cornelius considers him a messenger of God and falls at his feet in homage. But Peter graciously instructs Cornelius to stand up because he faces a fellow human being (verse 26). Whatever Peter has to offer this Gentile officer, it does not come from himself.

At the house of Cornelius, God is breaking down the barriers that for so long have been assumed to be God's will. Peter tells the assembly of the risk he is taking: "You yourselves know that it is unlawful for a Jew to associate with or to visit a Gentile" (verse 28). The Jews had erected firm barriers against Gentiles because of the need to maintain the purity of their beliefs and worship and to prevent them from being infiltrated by pagan doctrines and practices. But Peter goes on to explain that God has revised his understanding: "God has shown me that I should not call anyone profane or unclean." Peter now realizes that the barriers between Jews and Gentiles no longer serve their original purpose, as God is bringing about a new age of salvation for all in Jesus Christ.

Peter's sermon is the last example of his preaching in Acts, and it is his only speech addressed to a Gentile audience. He begins with a stunning proclamation: "I truly understand that God shows no partiality" (verse 34). God treats everyone on the same basis, and people from every nation have the same potential access to God. Peter highlights only two characteristics of the person who is acceptable to God: "anyone who fears him and does what is right" (verse 35). In other words, those who treat God with reverence and treat people with justice are ready for the saving revelation of God through Jesus Christ. This monumental statement of God's non-partiality among those he calls to faith reverberates down through the history of the church. God sends the Holy Spirit upon all who accept the good news, and God forbids human partiality or prejudice from limiting his saving work. ·

The proclamation of the good news of Jesus Christ is effective for those who are ready to receive it. It becomes a saving message for those who are open and realize their need for God. Cornelius had been seeking God for a long time. He has already begun to pray and to do good for those in need. God has been preparing his mind and heart for the message he is now receiving from Peter. Through the preached gospel, Cornelius moves from an open seeker to a confirmed believer.

Summarizing the essentials of the Christian message, Peter emphasizes that Jesus is "Lord of all" (verse 36). The great commission given by Jesus to his disciples, to preach the message of salvation "to all nations, beginning in Jerusalem" (Luke 24:47), is beginning to be realized as the saving news extends beyond Jerusalem and is destined for all the nations of the world.

As Peter is still speaking, proclaiming forgiveness of sins to everyone who believes, the Holy Spirit is given to Cornelius and the other Gentiles who are listening to Peter (verse 44). The Jewish believers who have come with Peter are amazed that "the gift of the Holy Spirit" has been poured out "even on the Gentiles" (verse 45). The coming of God's promised Spirit is the sign of the new era, and this event has rightly been called the Pentecost of the Gentile world (verse 47).

Peter understands the significance of the moment and he instructs that the Gentiles be baptized in the name of Jesus Christ (verse 48). Jews and Gentiles are equal in Christ; their need and God's answer to that need is the same. Peter receives hospitality and shares table fellowship for several days with these uncircumcised Christians. He is God's primary instrument of this epoch-making work, showing that the Gentiles too are chosen for salvation, baptism, and membership in Christ's church. The way has been prepared for the gospel to go out into the entire world.

Reflection and discussion

• Why does Luke show that the meeting between Peter and Cornelius is a climactic moment in the development of Acts? How is their encounter a critical moment for the early church?

• The Spirit of God is about the business of tearing down barriers that divide people. What walls of prejudice and bias prevent the gospel from being truly universal today?

Prayer

Lord of all, you taught your church to transcend nations, races, genders, and all divisions. You know the ways in which my mind and heart need conversion. Lead me to see other people as you see them, and to offer them the love that you have for them.

"If then God gave them the same gift that he gave us when we believed in the Lord Jesus Christ, who was I that I could hinder God?" Acts 11:17

Peter's Report to the Church in Jerusalem

ACTS 11:1-18 *¹Now the apostles and the believers who were in Judea heard that the Gentiles had also accepted the word of God. ²So when Peter went up to Jerusalem, the circumcised believers criticized him, ³saying, "Why did you go to uncircumcised men and eat with them?" ⁴Then Peter began to explain it to them, step by step, saying, ⁵"I was in the city of Joppa praying, and in a trance I saw a vision. There was something like a large sheet coming down from heaven, being lowered by its four corners; and it came close to me. ⁶As I looked at it closely I saw four-footed animals, beasts of prey, reptiles, and birds of the air. ⁷I also heard a voice saying to me, 'Get up, Peter; kill and eat.' ⁸But I replied, 'By no means, Lord; for nothing profane or unclean has ever entered my mouth.' ⁹But a second time the voice answered from heaven, 'What God has made clean, you must not call profane.' ¹⁰This happened three times; then everything was pulled up again to heaven. ¹¹At that very moment three men, sent to me from Caesarea, arrived at the house where we were. ¹²The Spirit told me to go with them and not to make a distinction between them and us. These six brothers also accompanied me, and we entered the man's house. ¹³He told us how he had seen the angel standing in his house and saying, 'Send to Joppa and bring Simon, who is called Peter; ¹⁴he will give you a message by which you and your entire* *household will be saved.' [15]And as I began to speak, the Holy Spirit fell upon them just as it had upon us at the beginning. [16]And I remembered the word of the Lord, how he had said, 'John baptized with water, but you will be baptized with the Holy Spirit.' [17]If then God gave them the same gift that he gave us when we believed in the Lord Jesus Christ, who was I that I could hinder God?" [18]When they heard this, they were silenced. And they praised God, saying, "Then God has given even to the Gentiles the repentance that leads to life."*

T he final scene of the account of Gentile conversion takes place in Jerusalem. Although it is largely a retelling of the story from Peter's point of view, its purpose is to establish the link between the church of the apostles in Jerusalem and the new mission to the Gentiles. There is no doubt that many Jewish Christians in Jerusalem would find such a revolutionary move controversial, so this scene presents a defense of its legitimacy and a justification for this new possibility for spreading the gospel. Peter is the bridge builder between the apostles in Jerusalem and the new expansion of the church beyond the boundaries of Judaism.

The apostles and Jewish believers in Jerusalem hear that the Gentiles have "accepted the word of God," welcoming the gospel message with their hearts. But when Peter arrives back in Jerusalem, some among the Hebrew Christians, "the circumcised," criticize him for eating with Gentiles, "the uncircumcised," disobeying the rules for purity and diet. In their view, any Gentile who wishes to join the believing community must follow the prescriptions of the covenant God made with Israel, including circumcision and following the provisions of the law. In response, Peter explains "step by step" what has happened, beginning with his vision and continuing through the conversion and baptism of Cornelius and his household.

The chief aim of the narrative is to convince the reader that what happened through Peter is truly God's action through the work of the Holy Spirit. Peter says that his vision happened three times and concluded with the explanatory voice from heaven, "What God has made clean, you must not call profane." Immediately the three men sent by Cornelius arrived and the Holy Spirit instructed Peter not only to travel with them but "not to make a distinction between them and us" (verse 12). The expression means that Peter must exercise no partiality against them because they are Gentiles. So with six Christian brothers as witnesses, Peter went to the house of Cornelius, just as the Spirit directed.

As Peter proclaimed the gospel to Cornelius and his household, the Holy Spirit came upon them. Peter notes that the Spirit came upon these Gentiles just as the Spirit had come upon the apostles and the Jewish Christians at Pentecost (verse 15). That the same manifestation of the Spirit is given to them as was received by the apostles is the greatest indicator that God is giving salvation to the Gentiles (verse 17). This testimony of Peter to the church in Jerusalem causes the believers to praise God, rejoicing that God has given life to the Gentiles too (verse 18).

When Jesus gave Peter the authority to lead his church, Jesus enabled him to guide the practices of the community in ways which would have far-reaching consequences. This critical section of Acts shows that Peter is indeed the authoritative guide within the early church as he is moved by the assurance of God's Spirit to open the way of faith to the Gentiles. Though the apostolic mission to all parts of the world would soon be led by Paul, the apostle to the Gentiles, this narrative makes it clear that Peter was the inaugurator of this mission. Paul's missionary activity could take place only after Peter's inspired and decisive action opened the door.

Reflection and discussion

• What is the reason for the change in attitude among the Jewish Christians as shown from verse 2 to verse 18? What seems to be the decisive factor that leads from criticism to acceptance?

• Why would God have chosen Peter to be the first to go to the Gentiles? In what way does Peter's entering the house of Cornelius demonstrate the importance of his role in the infant church?

• How does Peter's action prepare the way for Paul? Why can Paul's missionary activity take place only after Peter's inspired and decisive action opens the door?

• The church is called to be one, holy, catholic, and apostolic. How does Peter's experience with Cornelius express these marks of the church?

Prayer

Lord of all people, you made Peter the bridge builder between the Jews and the Gentiles. Thank you for the unifying ministry of Peter among the community of believers. Make me an instrument of unity for your church.

So it was that for an entire year they met with the church and taught a great many people, and it was in Antioch that the disciples were first called "Christians." Acts 11:26

Barnabas and Saul in Antioch

ACTS 11:19-30 *¹⁹Now those who were scattered because of the persecution that took place over Stephen traveled as far as Phoenicia, Cyprus, and Antioch, and they spoke the word to no one except Jews. ²⁰But among them were some men of Cyprus and Cyrene who, on coming to Antioch, spoke to the Hellenists also, proclaiming the Lord Jesus. ²¹The hand of the Lord was with them, and a great number became believers and turned to the Lord. ²²News of this came to the ears of the church in Jerusalem, and they sent Barnabas to Antioch. ²³When he came and saw the grace of God, he rejoiced, and he exhorted them all to remain faithful to the Lord with steadfast devotion; ²⁴for he was a good man, full of the Holy Spirit and of faith. And a great many people were brought to the Lord. ²⁵Then Barnabas went to Tarsus to look for Saul, ²⁶and when he had found him, he brought him to Antioch. So it was that for an entire year they met with the church and taught a great many people, and it was in Antioch that the disciples were first called "Christians."*

²⁷At that time prophets came down from Jerusalem to Antioch. ²⁸One of them named Agabus stood up and predicted by the Spirit that there would be a severe famine over all the world; and this took place during the reign of Claudius. ²⁹The disciples determined that according to their ability, each would send relief to the believers living in Judea; [30]*this they did, sending it to the elders by Barnabas and Saul.*

As a result of the persecution and scattering that followed Stephen's martyrdom, the church continued to expand to more distant places. Luke mentions the expansion to Phoenicia, the seacoast area of Syria, and to Cyprus, an island to the south of Asia Minor with a large Jewish colony. But his main focus is Antioch, a large metropolitan city in Syria (today located in southeastern Turkey). Rome, Alexandria, and Antioch were the largest cities of the Greco-Roman world. In each of these great cities, there was a sizable Jewish population, but the vast majority of the population was Gentile. Although the missionaries from Jerusalem proclaimed the gospel only to the Jewish population of Antioch, other missionaries spoke the good news of Jesus also to the Greek-speaking Gentiles.

Because of its mixed population and variety of cultures, Antioch was the ideal location for beginning to break down the dividing wall between Jews and Gentiles. The city was full of religious activity, and many gods were worshipped there. Judaism functioned as an exception in adhering to belief in the one true God. Because the mission to the Gentiles was guided by God, "a great number became believers and turned to the Lord" (verse 21). The church in Antioch then launched its own mission, reaching out into the larger world to proclaim the gospel and extend the church. In time, Antioch became one of the great centers of learning and governance for the ancient church.

When the church in Jerusalem hears about the growth in Antioch, it sends Barnabas to investigate what is happening there and to establish a relationship with the new believers. Upon his arrival, Barnabas rejoices to see the evidence of God's grace, and he urges the new disciples "to remain faithful to the Lord with steadfast devotion" (verse 23). Always "the son of encouragement" as his name implies, Barnabas shows himself to be "full of the Holy Spirit and of faith" (verse 24). He seems to have become a leader in the church at Antioch because of his personal qualities and his long association with the apostles. Through his efforts and those of the other missionaries, "a great many people were brought to the Lord."

As the church grew in Antioch, Barnabas realizes that he needs help in building up the community of disciples there. He goes to Tarsus to search for Saul and, finding him, Barnabas brings him back to Antioch with him. For a full year, they work together, instructing the church in Antioch as the apostles were doing in Jerusalem (verse 26). As a result of their ministry and of the distinct identity of this church of both Jewish and Gentile believers, Luke tells us that "it was in Antioch that the disciples were first called 'Christians.'" So in addition to being called "saints," "believers," and "disciples," they began here to be called Christians.

Barnabas was not the only link between the church in Jerusalem and Antioch. Those who came from Jerusalem to Antioch included prophets, those who had the gift of preaching God's revelation and expressing God's will. The prophet Agabus predicts a severe famine throughout the Roman world. Because this famine would be particularly difficult for the believers in Judea, the disciples in Antioch determine that they would send relief to the needy in Jerusalem. Barnabas and Saul deliver the support to the elders who serve the church in Jerusalem. The aid is another expression of the church's unity and charity across geographical and ethnic boundaries.

Reflection and discussion

• What seem to be some of the reasons for the rapid growth of Christianity in Antioch?

• Why did the distinctive name of "Christian" develop for the believers in Antioch? What are the implications of that title for me?

• What are some of the ways that the apostles and elders in Jerusalem maintained unity with the new and growing church in Antioch? Why was it so important to maintain the oneness of the church?

• What are some of the qualities of Barnabas that make him an ideal missionary for the gospel?

• What am I learning from Acts about the church's call to evangelization and about my own role in that mission?

Prayer

Lord Jesus, I proudly call myself a Christian and confess this title as my primary identity. Keep me united with other believers, and help me to manifest the truth, goodness, and beauty of your church in the words and deeds of my own life.

SUGGESTIONS FOR FACILITATORS, GROUP SESSION 5

1. Welcome group members and ask if anyone has any questions, announcements, or requests.

2. You may want to pray this prayer as a group:

   God of all nations, you desire the salvation of all people and you reveal yourself through Jesus to the people of the covenant and to the Gentiles of the world. Continue to teach us how to transcend barriers and differences that divide people, so that your church may be one in Christ. You transformed the apostles Peter and Paul to serve your church as its sustaining pillars, and you made them evangelizers to Jews and Gentiles. May the ministry of Peter, the bridge builder, and the ministry of Paul, the apostle to distant nations, continue to build up the church in unity and in love.

3. Ask one or more of the following questions:
   • What most intrigued you from this week's study?
   • What makes you want to know and understand more of God's word?

4. Discuss lessons 19 through 24. Choose one or more of the questions for reflection and discussion from each lesson to talk over as a group.

5. Ask the group members to name one thing they have most appreciated about the way the group has worked during this Bible study. Ask group members to discuss any changes they might suggest in the way the group works in future studies.

6. Invite group members to complete lessons 25 through 30 on their own during the six days before the next meeting. They should write out their own answers to the questions as preparation for next week's session.

7. Ask group members what they find most fascinating about the church in the Acts of the Apostles. Discuss some of these insights in Luke's presentation of the church.

8. Conclude by praying aloud together the prayer at the end of one of the lessons discussed. You may want to conclude the prayer by asking members to voice prayers of thanksgiving.

Suddenly an angel of the Lord appeared and a light shone in the cell.
He tapped Peter on the side and woke him, saying, "Get up quickly."
And the chains fell off his wrists. Acts 12:7

Persecution and Deliverance in Jerusalem

ACTS 12:1-25 *¹About that time King Herod laid violent hands upon some who belonged to the church. ²He had James, the brother of John, killed with the sword. ³After he saw that it pleased the Jews, he proceeded to arrest Peter also. (This was during the festival of Unleavened Bread.) ⁴When he had seized him, he put him in prison and handed him over to four squads of soldiers to guard him, intending to bring him out to the people after the Passover. ⁵While Peter was kept in prison, the church prayed fervently to God for him. ⁶The very night before Herod was going to bring him out, Peter, bound with two chains, was sleeping between two soldiers, while guards in front of the door were keeping watch over the prison. ⁷Suddenly an angel of the Lord appeared and a light shone in the cell. He tapped Peter on the side and woke him, saying, "Get up quickly." And the chains fell off his wrists. ⁸The angel said to him, "Fasten your belt and put on your sandals." He did so. Then he said to him, "Wrap your cloak around you and follow me." ⁹Peter went out and followed him; he did not realize that what was happening with the angel's help was real; he thought he was seeing a vision. ¹⁰After they had passed the first and the second guard, they came before the iron gate leading into the city. It opened for them of its own accord, and they* went outside and walked along a lane, when suddenly the angel left him. [11]Then Peter came to himself and said, "Now I am sure that the Lord has sent his angel and rescued me from the hands of Herod and from all that the Jewish people were expecting."

[12]As soon as he realized this, he went to the house of Mary, the mother of John whose other name was Mark, where many had gathered and were praying. [13]When he knocked at the outer gate, a maid named Rhoda came to answer. [14]On recognizing Peter's voice, she was so overjoyed that, instead of opening the gate, she ran in and announced that Peter was standing at the gate. [15]They said to her, "You are out of your mind!" But she insisted that it was so. They said, "It is his angel." [16]Meanwhile Peter continued knocking; and when they opened the gate, they saw him and were amazed. [17]He motioned to them with his hand to be silent, and described for them how the Lord had brought him out of the prison. And he added, "Tell this to James and to the believers." Then he left and went to another place.

[18]When morning came, there was no small commotion among the soldiers over what had become of Peter. [19]When Herod had searched for him and could not find him, he examined the guards and ordered them to be put to death. Then he went down from Judea to Caesarea and stayed there.

[20]Now Herod was angry with the people of Tyre and Sidon. So they came to him in a body; and after winning over Blastus, the king's chamberlain, they asked for a reconciliation, because their country depended on the king's country for food. [21]On an appointed day Herod put on his royal robes, took his seat on the platform, and delivered a public address to them. [22]The people kept shouting, "The voice of a god, and not of a mortal!" [23]And immediately, because he had not given the glory to God, an angel of the Lord struck him down, and he was eaten by worms and died.

[24]But the word of God continued to advance and gain adherents. [25]Then after completing their mission Barnabas and Saul returned to Jerusalem and brought with them John, whose other name was Mark.

The persecution of the church in Jerusalem continues to intensify, from the religious authorities and then from the government of Herod Agrippa, the grandson of Herod the Great. Knowing that Herod Agrippa ruled over Judea from AD 41 to 44 helps us to date these events. The ruler seeks to annihilate the Christian movement and so strikes at its highest leadership. He has James the apostle beheaded with a sword, and he targets Peter with the same fate. Peter is arrested and imprisoned during the same Jewish feast on which Jesus was put to death. Herod plans to bring Peter before the people after Passover to face judgment and be executed.

Peter is held in maximum security, with one soldier chained to each of his arms and two others guarding the door. Meanwhile, the church is praying fervently for him (verse 5). At the last moment, the night before Peter is to appear for judgment, God acts through the ministry of an angel to rescue him (verses 6-7). With a shining light, God rescues him from the darkness, and liberates him from imminent death. Peter emerges from the prison alive, and he goes off to tell the disciples the good news.

Peter goes immediately to the house where the disciples were meeting and knocks on the door. With comic detail, the writer describes how the servant girl, Rhoda, is so excited when she realizes it is Peter that she forgets to open the door and let him in (verses 13-14). Instead, she rushes off to tell the community of believers who are gathered inside. While they argue for a while over Rhoda's sanity, Peter continues to knock at the door. Peter has a harder time getting into the house of the believing community than he had getting out of prison. An angel led him out of Herod's cell, but he cannot get through the locked gate of the disciples. When he is finally allowed in the house, Peter tells the astonished crowd what has happened.

There are clear parallels between Peter's ordeal and the passion and resurrection of Jesus: both occur at Passover (verses 3-4); Peter's emergence from prison resembles Jesus' emergence from the tomb; and in both cases the disciples fail to believe the news brought by a woman. The escape of Peter from prison demonstrates that the resurrection of Jesus continues to empower his apostles. The pattern of God's action in Jesus remains the pattern for God's action in his followers. In the midst of hardship, God continues to offer new life.

Luke adds more humor to the scene as he helps us imagine the confusion of the guards the next morning (verse 18). Each blaming the other, they are flabbergasted by the empty chains beside them. Quite a commotion is raised as Herod searches for Peter and cannot find his prized prisoner. Luke contrasts the scenes of the believers in the house of John Mark and the baffled guards in the prison. The one is a scene of bewildered joy and gratitude; the other a scene of revenge and punishment. While the Christians praise God for

Peter's deliverance, the Roman guards are going to their death.

The escalating persecution and the desire of the authorities to kill Peter explain why he leaves his leadership position of the church in Jerusalem and goes "to another place" (verse 17). His parting words are a request to explain to James, the brother of Jesus, and the rest of the believers what has happened. This James will become the leading figure in the Jerusalem church, while Peter becomes a traveling missionary, basing his activity in Antioch.

The episode concludes by contrasting the gruesome judgment of Herod and the bounteous blessings of the church. Herod is struck dead, presumably for opposing the church and for receiving the people's praise, not giving the glory to God (verse 23). The church, however, despite its persecution, flourishes: "The word of God continued to advance and gain adherents" (verse 24). The scene now shifts from Jerusalem to Antioch and beyond.

Reflection and discussion

• Surely the church in Jerusalem prayed for the release of James the apostle just as it prayed for Peter's release. Why would God allow James to be martyred while he delivered Peter from imprisonment and death?

• Luke continually shows us how the life, death, and resurrection of Jesus is reflected and renewed within the church. In what ways does this account demonstrate that the power of Christ's saving death and resurrection is at work in the ministry of Peter?

• Peter was freed from prison because he responded to God's lead. In what aspect of my life should I admit my own powerlessness and surrender to the Highest Power to show me the way?

• Why would the Christian community delight in telling this story for many years? How does humor add to the enjoyment of this account?

• Do readers today see the humor in this account before it is explained to them? Why, or why not? How does Luke use humor to teach lessons to the disciples?

Prayer

Liberating God, thank you for the ways you have freed me from oppressive power that I am unable to control. Help me to trust in you, to live with gratitude, and to believe that you want to do marvelous things in my life.

**While they were worshiping the Lord and fasting,
the Holy Spirit said, "Set apart for me Barnabas and Saul
for the work to which I have called them."** Acts 13:2

Barnabas and Saul Commissioned to Evangelize

ACTS 13:1-12 *¹Now in the church at Antioch there were prophets and teachers: Barnabas, Simeon who was called Niger, Lucius of Cyrene, Manaen a member of the court of Herod the ruler, and Saul. ²While they were worshiping the Lord and fasting, the Holy Spirit said, "Set apart for me Barnabas and Saul for the work to which I have called them." ³Then after fasting and praying they laid their hands on them and sent them off.*

⁴So, being sent out by the Holy Spirit, they went down to Seleucia; and from there they sailed to Cyprus. ⁵When they arrived at Salamis, they proclaimed the word of God in the synagogues of the Jews. And they had John also to assist them. ⁶When they had gone through the whole island as far as Paphos, they met a certain magician, a Jewish false prophet, named Bar-Jesus. ⁷He was with the proconsul, Sergius Paulus, an intelligent man, who summoned Barnabas and Saul and wanted to hear the word of God. ⁸But the magician Elymas (for that is the translation of his name) opposed them and tried to turn the proconsul away from the faith. ⁹But Saul, also known as Paul, filled with the Holy Spirit, looked intently at him [10]and said, "You son of the devil, you enemy of all righteousness, full of all deceit and villainy, will you not stop making crooked the straight paths of the Lord? [11]And now listen—the hand of the Lord is against you, and you will be blind for a while, unable to see the sun." Immediately mist and darkness came over him, and he went about groping for someone to lead him by the hand. [12]When the proconsul saw what had happened, he believed, for he was astonished at the teaching about the Lord.

Attention turns to the church in Antioch and beyond. For the first time, a church other than the one in Jerusalem is the center for a major divine initiative. Jesus' call to witness the gospel "to the ends of the earth" has spurred a mission that is moving forward in earnest. Many centers of activity will emerge in addition to Jerusalem and Antioch because of the enormous scope of the work ahead. The church in Antioch shows that worship and mission together are the key tasks of the church. Antioch is the ancient model of the church's call to look beyond its own community to evangelize. Churches are established to go inward to worship God and to go outward in mission to others.

The church in Antioch is full of prophets and teachers witnessing to the gospel and discerning the call of the Holy Spirit. The teaching and prophetic activities of the young churches involve preaching the message of Jesus and passing on the apostolic teaching in the form of hymns, short doctrinal summaries, and rituals like baptism and Eucharist. The call of Barnabas and Saul takes place in the context of communal worship, with prayer and fasting. The Spirit directs that the two be sent out from the larger community for a special work. On the basis of their contribution to the church in Antioch they are qualified to begin establishing new Christian communities in other places. The urging of the Holy Spirit and the discernment of the church are met by the church's obedience to God's will. The calling of Barnabas and Saul is affirmed as the leaders lay their hands on them and send them forth from the assembly.

This first missionary journey is initiated and directed by the Holy Spirit. Seleucia is the port city for Antioch, and the nearby island of Cyprus is the first stop on the mission trail. Barnabas and Paul, also accompanied by John Mark, travel the entire length of this large island, from its eastern port at

Salamis and its western port at Paphos. As will be Paul's custom throughout Acts, they begin preaching in the Jewish synagogues throughout Cyprus. At Paphos, the missionaries encounter a Jewish false prophet and magician named Elymas Bar-Jesus (verse 6). He is in the company of the Roman pro-consul, Sergius Paulus, who must have used the magician to search for signs using magical formulas, charms, and incantations. But Sergius wants to hear the word of God proclaimed by Barnabas and Paul, and Elymus opposes the preaching of the missionaries, probably out of fear for his own position, and tries to keep Sergius from the faith.

Saul, now known by his Roman name Paul, acts under the Spirit's guidance and functions as a true prophet in contrast to the magician. He looks intently at Elymas, delivers a strong judgment against him, and renders him temporarily blind (verses 9-11). The magician's deceitfulness and villainy pervert the truth and make God's path crooked. As he sits in darkness, he must reflect on the source of God's power and truth. The episode contrasts Paul, who was also temporarily blinded but is now filled with the truth and the Spirit, with the blind Elymas, groping in the mist and darkness. We also see a contrast between Elymus, who struggles against the faith, and Sergius, who is open to the gospel and is astonished by Paul's teaching. We are not told what happens to Elymus, though we can hope for his conversion, but we are told that Sergius responds with faith and becomes a believer.

Reflection and discussion

• Why must churches be both inward-directed and outward-directed? How do communities determine a balance between worship and mission?

• Paul seems to have two different missionary approaches: one to Elymas who opposes the gospel, and another to Sergius who is open to Paul's teaching. What can the church learn from Paul's different styles for each one?

• Why did Elymas try to turn Sergius from the faith? When and how have people tried to turn me from the faith?

• What is the evidence that a Christian community is guided by the Holy Spirit? What is the relationship between the Spirit's guidance and the church's authorization for ministry and mission?

Prayer

Holy Spirit, you directed the church to set apart Paul and Barnabas for their mission. Help me to experience your call and to discern the unique mission you have chosen for me. Direct and lead me in the straight paths of the Lord.

"And we bring you the good news that what God promised to our ancestors he has fulfilled for us, their children, by raising Jesus." Acts 13:32-33

Paul and Barnabas in Antioch of Pisidia

ACTS 13:13-41 *¹³Then Paul and his companions set sail from Paphos and came to Perga in Pamphylia. John, however, left them and returned to Jerusalem; ¹⁴but they went on from Perga and came to Antioch in Pisidia. And on the sabbath day they went into the synagogue and sat down. ¹⁵After the reading of the law and the prophets, the officials of the synagogue sent them a message, saying, "Brothers, if you have any word of exhortation for the people, give it." ¹⁶So Paul stood up and with a gesture began to speak:*

"You Israelites, and others who fear God, listen. ¹⁷The God of this people Israel chose our ancestors and made the people great during their stay in the land of Egypt, and with uplifted arm he led them out of it. ¹⁸For about forty years he put up with them in the wilderness. ¹⁹After he had destroyed seven nations in the land of Canaan, he gave them their land as an inheritance ²⁰for about four hundred fifty years. After that he gave them judges until the time of the prophet Samuel. ²¹Then they asked for a king; and God gave them Saul son of Kish, a man of the tribe of Benjamin, who reigned for forty years. ²²When he had removed him, he made David their king. In his testimony about him he said, 'I

have found David, son of Jesse, to be a man after my heart, who will carry out all my wishes.' [23] Of this man's posterity God has brought to Israel a Savior, Jesus, as he promised; [24] before his coming John had already proclaimed a baptism of repentance to all the people of Israel. [25] And as John was finishing his work, he said, 'What do you suppose that I am? I am not he. No, but one is coming after me; I am not worthy to untie the thong of the sandals on his feet.'

[26] "My brothers, you descendants of Abraham's family, and others who fear God, to us the message of this salvation has been sent. [27] Because the residents of Jerusalem and their leaders did not recognize him or understand the words of the prophets that are read every sabbath, they fulfilled those words by condemning him. [28] Even though they found no cause for a sentence of death, they asked Pilate to have him killed. [29] When they had carried out everything that was written about him, they took him down from the tree and laid him in a tomb. [30] But God raised him from the dead; [31] and for many days he appeared to those who came up with him from Galilee to Jerusalem, and they are now his witnesses to the people. [32] And we bring you the good news that what God promised to our ancestors [33] he has fulfilled for us, their children, by raising Jesus; as also it is written in the second psalm,

'You are my Son;
    today I have begotten you.'

[34] As to his raising him from the dead, no more to return to corruption, he has spoken in this way,

'I will give you the holy promises made to David.'

[35] Therefore he has also said in another psalm,

'You will not let your Holy One experience corruption.'

[36] For David, after he had served the purpose of God in his own generation, died, was laid beside his ancestors, and experienced corruption; [37] but he whom God raised up experienced no corruption. [38] Let it be known to you therefore, my brothers, that through this man forgiveness of sins is proclaimed to you; [39] by this Jesus everyone who believes is set free from all those sins from which you could not be freed by the law of Moses. [40] Beware, therefore, that what the prophets said does not happen to you:

[41] 'Look, you scoffers!
    Be amazed and perish,
for in your days I am doing a work,
    a work that you will never believe, even if someone tells you.'"

T he travel itinerary of Paul and his companions becomes increasingly grueling. They journey by ship from Paphos on the coast of Cyprus to Perga in southern Asia Minor. They then travel northward through the mountainous region to Antioch in Pisidia. Here they attend the synagogue service, as was their practice in every town on their journey. After readings from the Torah and the prophets, the synagogue officials invite the travelers to speak to the people, offering "a word of exhortation." As Paul arises to accept the invitation, he addresses a mixed group of Jews and "others who fear God," that is, Gentiles who are interested in Judaism.

This first sermon of Paul in Acts is typical of his rabbinical style of interpreting recent events in light of Israel's ancient Scriptures. He offers a broad sweep of Israel's saving history in order to show how God has acted again to definitively liberate Israel through Jesus the Savior. He identifies with his audience by speaking about "our ancestors" and the unique covenant relationship God made with them. He recounts the most familiar features: the exodus from Egypt (verse 17), the testing in the wilderness (verse 18), the conquest of the land (verse 19), the period of the judges (verse 20), and the monarchy under Saul and David (verses 21-22).

After leading up to the reign of King David, Paul's narrative leaps over a thousand years of history to David's descendant, the new king of God's people, the promised Savior (verse 23). John the Baptist is the last link in Israel's history before the Messiah's coming, the bridge between the promises and their fulfillment. And now, Paul proclaims, "to us the message of this salvation has been sent" (verse 26). He warns that the people of Jerusalem failed to recognize their Savior because they did not understand the words of the prophets that pointed to him. Instead, they condemned him and handed him over to Pilate to be killed, fulfilling the words of the prophets themselves (verses 27-29). Yet, God raised Jesus from the tomb of death, and he appeared to his disciples, who are now his witnesses.

"What God promised" is expressed through the ancient Scriptures of Israel, and what God "has fulfilled" is expressed through the life, death, and resurrection of Jesus (verses 32-33). Paul cites ancient texts from the psalms that originally referred to David and shows his audience that what God promised David is now given to the present generation in Jesus. The Messiah's resurrection is the complete fulfillment of God's promise to raise up an eternal heir to the throne of David. Contrasting what is possible "by the law of Moses" with what can be achieved through Jesus, Paul declares that through Jesus forgiveness and freedom from sin is given to everyone who believes (verses 38-39). Finally, Paul ends his exhortation by warning his hearers with a quote from the prophet Habakkuk (verses 40-41). In the days of the prophet, the people failed to recognize what was happening as the work of God. Paul tells his audience in the synagogue that they must not scoff at the message of the gospel they are hearing but must respond with faith in Christ.

Reflection and discussion

• What impels Paul to travel on such unrelentingly difficult journeys? In what ways does he inspire me with his zeal for the gospel?

• Why does Paul's exhortation in the synagogue highlight moments from Israel's history in order to help his hearers understand what God has done in Jesus Christ?

• How does the resurrection of Jesus confirm the fullest meaning of the four Scripture quotations from which Paul quotes?

Prayer

God of Moses, David, and all the prophets, inspire me and give me courage through the stories of my ancestors in faith. Show me how Jesus your Son is the answer to all your covenant promises to Israel.

"It was necessary that the word of God should be spoken first to you. Since you reject it and judge yourselves to be unworthy of eternal life, we are now turning to the Gentiles." Acts 13:46

Paul and Barnabas Turn to the Gentiles

ACTS 13:42-52 *⁴²As Paul and Barnabas were going out, the people urged them to speak about these things again the next sabbath. ⁴³When the meeting of the synagogue broke up, many Jews and devout converts to Judaism followed Paul and Barnabas, who spoke to them and urged them to continue in the grace of God.*

⁴⁴The next sabbath almost the whole city gathered to hear the word of the Lord. ⁴⁵But when the Jews saw the crowds, they were filled with jealousy; and blaspheming, they contradicted what was spoken by Paul. ⁴⁶Then both Paul and Barnabas spoke out boldly, saying, "It was necessary that the word of God should be spoken first to you. Since you reject it and judge yourselves to be unworthy of eternal life, we are now turning to the Gentiles. ⁴⁷For so the Lord has commanded us, saying,

'I have set you to be a light for the Gentiles,
so that you may bring salvation to the ends of the earth.'"

⁴⁸When the Gentiles heard this, they were glad and praised the word of the Lord; and as many as had been destined for eternal life became believers. ⁴⁹Thus the word of the Lord spread throughout the region. ⁵⁰But the Jews incited the devout women of high standing and the leading men of the city, and stirred up persecution against Paul and Barnabas, and drove them out of their region. [51]So they shook the dust off their feet in protest against them, and went to Iconium. [52]And the disciples were filled with joy and with the Holy Spirit.

A s Paul preaches from town to town, going first to the synagogues on the Sabbath, Paul never separates himself from his own people, the Jews. He seeks to bring the message of salvation to the Israelites scattered to all the nations throughout the world. He places himself among Israel's ancestors, rejoicing in their divine election, grateful for the covenant promises offered to them, and filled with grief at their unfaithfulness to God. He proclaims the gospel as the fulfillment of the Torah and the prophets, and he knows that the response of his audience will determine its destination. Repeatedly, Paul's preaching of the good news of Jesus, connected with the Scriptures of Israel, is called "the word of the Lord."

Paul's speech in Antioch of Pisidia receives a positive response, and the people urge him to return the next Sabbath. Many Jews follow Paul, and he urges them to "continue in the grace of God" (verses 42-43). On the next Sabbath, almost the whole city gathers to hear "the word of the Lord." But the huge crowds stir many of the Jewish leaders to jealousy, and they object to the way the Gentiles are being connected to Israel's God. They oppose Paul, contradict his inclusive message, and stir up a persecution against him. Their zeal for the covenant has blinded them to the scope of God's will, preventing them from seeing how God's promises are being fulfilled in this breakthrough to all the nations.

In response, Paul speaks out boldly, demonstrating how his mission from the Lord is a response to the words of Isaiah: "I have set you to be a light to the Gentiles, so that you may bring salvation to the ends of the earth" (verse 47). This ancient prophecy of God's saving plan for the nations is fulfilled in Jesus and extended through his church and the work of Paul. God has commanded Barnabas and Paul to be a guiding light to the nations concerning the way to God. The goal of God's plan is to take the message of salvation in Jesus Christ to the ends of the earth, to extend it to all nations in every part of the world.

In contrast to the rejection the apostles receive among many of the Jews, the

Gentiles are delighted when they hear Paul's preaching, and they praise "the word of the Lord" (verse 48). So, from this point on, Paul turns increasingly to the Gentiles, although he never turns his back on the people of Israel. In nearly every city of his travels, he goes first to the Jews, and when turned away by one synagogue, he goes to another. He knows that the covenant benefits were promised first to his own people, and he never ceases to identify himself with them. Yet, through his mission to the Gentiles, he makes explicit what was implicit in God's plan all along—to bring the message of salvation to all the nations of the earth. Increasingly from this point on, the narrative of Acts will focus on the mission to the Gentiles and almost exclusively on the work of Paul.

Reflection and discussion

• How many times in this passage is the message Paul spoke referred to as "the word of the Lord"? Why does Luke give Paul's preaching the same status as the ancient Scriptures of Israel?

• The scene from Acts shows a variety of emotional responses created by Paul's proclamation of "the word of the Lord" among the various groups in the city. Why does Paul's message produce such a variety of reactions? What are the responses generated by the word of the Lord today?

• Why were Paul's Jewish hearers the most resistant to his message? Why does Paul continue to make evangelization among the Jews his first priority?

• Through the faith and zeal of the apostles, the church grew rapidly from its small beginnings in Jerusalem. What are some of the reasons for its rapid growth throughout the Roman Empire?

• While traveling from city to city, Paul and Barnabas are "filled with joy and the Holy Spirit" (verse 52), despite the rejection and persecution they experience. What does their lack of discouragement indicate about their mission? How is it possible to avoid discouragement when doing the work of the Lord?

Prayer

Saving God, you have raised up Jesus as a light for all the nations so that salvation will come to all peoples. Enable me to listen carefully to your word, and let me know what part of your church's mission you want me to fulfill today. Help me to know those things that I ought to do and those things that I must patiently leave in your hands.

The priest of Zeus, whose temple was just outside the city, brought oxen and garlands to the gates; he and the crowds wanted to offer sacrifice. Acts 14:13

Paul and Barnabas Honored as Greek Gods

ACTS 14:1-20 *¹The same thing occurred in Iconium, where Paul and Barnabas went into the Jewish synagogue and spoke in such a way that a great number of both Jews and Greeks became believers. ²But the unbelieving Jews stirred up the Gentiles and poisoned their minds against the brothers. ³So they remained for a long time, speaking boldly for the Lord, who testified to the word of his grace by granting signs and wonders to be done through them. ⁴But the residents of the city were divided; some sided with the Jews, and some with the apostles. ⁵And when an attempt was made by both Gentiles and Jews, with their rulers, to mistreat them and to stone them, ⁶the apostles learned of it and fled to Lystra and Derbe, cities of Lycaonia, and to the surrounding country; ⁷and there they continued proclaiming the good news.*

⁸In Lystra there was a man sitting who could not use his feet and had never walked, for he had been crippled from birth. ⁹He listened to Paul as he was speaking. And Paul, looking at him intently and seeing that he had faith to be healed, ¹⁰said in a loud voice, "Stand upright on your feet." And the man sprang up and began to walk. ¹¹When the crowds saw what Paul had done, they shouted in the Lycaonian language, "The gods have come down to us in human form!" ¹²Barnabas they called Zeus, and Paul they called Hermes, because he

123

*was the chief speaker. *[13]*The priest of Zeus, whose temple was just outside the city, brought oxen and garlands to the gates; he and the crowds wanted to offer sacrifice. *[14]*When the apostles Barnabas and Paul heard of it, they tore their clothes and rushed out into the crowd, shouting, *[15]*"Friends, why are you doing this? We are mortals just like you, and we bring you good news, that you should turn from these worthless things to the living God, who made the heaven and the earth and the sea and all that is in them. *[16]*In past generations he allowed all the nations to follow their own ways; *[17]*yet he has not left himself without a witness in doing good—giving you rains from heaven and fruitful seasons, and filling you with food and your hearts with joy." *[18]*Even with these words, they scarcely restrained the crowds from offering sacrifice to them.*

*[19]*But Jews came there from Antioch and Iconium and won over the crowds. Then they stoned Paul and dragged him out of the city, supposing that he was dead. *[20]*But when the disciples surrounded him, he got up and went into the city. The next day he went on with Barnabas to Derbe.*

Paul and Barnabas continue their missionary journey, traveling from town to town along the Roman commercial roads in the area that is today central Turkey. Although Paul has declared that the mission is now directed to the Gentiles, they continue to go first to the synagogue in each town they visit. In Iconium, "a great number of both Jews and Greeks became believers." In contrast, some of the unbelieving Jews begin to oppose the missionaries and to work against their efforts to preach to the Gentiles. Yet, Paul and Barnabas decide to remain and continue their mission in the face of opposition. As they boldly speak for God "the word of his grace," God confirms their testimony with signs and wonders (verse 3). The city is divided: some are for the Jews who oppose the missionaries; others are for Paul and Barnabas, who are here described as "apostles" (verse 4). Only when these apostles discover a plot to assault and stone them do they flee to the next town.

In the town of Lystra, Paul's mission to evangelize the Gentiles becomes more explicit. There is no mention of a synagogue here, and Paul and Barnabas seem to encounter a purely Gentile audience. Paul proclaims the good news in the marketplace and there encounters a man who was crippled from birth. Paul's healing of the man resembles Peter's healing of the lame man at the temple (3:1-16), showing the complementary nature of the ministries of Peter and Paul. After listening to Paul speak, the lame man perceives God's power in his words, and he opens himself to God's transforming authority. The man's helplessness and inability to move on his own signify the human condition in need of salvation. He then expresses the trusting conviction of faith, and as Paul commands him to "stand upright," he experiences God's saving strength.

The response of the Gentile crowds to the healing is overwhelmingly positive (verses 10-12). Thinking that Barnabas is Zeus, the principal god of the Greeks, and Paul is Hermes, the messenger god who governs speech, the people express their gratitude for the saving message by means of their own pagan practices. The priest of the town brings oxen and garlands to perform a grand sacrifice for these gods in human form (verse 13). But when the news reaches Paul and Barnabas about what the people are doing, they tear their clothes in distress and rush to protest their action.

As the brief summary of Paul's address demonstrates, their missionary method to Gentiles is significantly different than their previous strategies. Rather than beginning with the Hebrew Scriptures as he had in the synagogue, Paul begins with philosophy and natural theology. Instead of showing that Jesus is the Messiah of Israel as he had with the Jews, he begins teaching about the one God who is the principal cause of all things. This "living God," he teaches, is the one who creates and sustains all things in existence (verse 15). The activity of God in nature—making the crops fruitful and bringing joy to human hearts—is a "witness" to God's goodness (verse 17). Paul explains that in the past God allowed all people to follow their own gods and beliefs. Now, however, is the time to offer the good news of the living God to all the nations.

The final scene shows that reception of Paul's preaching and intense opposition exist side by side. In the same city, there are those who wish to honor the apostles as gods and those who wish to put them to death. After some of Paul's Jewish opponents come from Antioch and Iconium and win over the crowds at Lystra, they stone Paul and drag him out of the city. Sometimes Paul discerns that it is best to stay put despite opposition, and at other times he knows that it is best to move on. Here, he and Barnabas move on to the town of Derbe, but they will return shortly to strengthen the believers, despite the danger.

Reflection and discussion

• In response to the people of Lystra who want to worship Paul and Barnabas, they insist, "We are mortals just like you." Why is it important to attribute power to its divine source rather than its human instruments?

• What are some of the differences between Paul's approach to the Jews and his approach to the Gentiles? What is the reason for different evangelizing strategies for different people?

• Do I experience God more in my personal history or in the wonders of the created world? What are the primary witnesses of God's existence for me?

Prayer

Maker of heaven and earth, you lovingly sustain all things in existence, and you give your creation all that is necessary for nourishment and gladness. Help me to trust in your bounty and to use your gifts for your greater glory and honor.

When they arrived, they called the church together
and related all that God had done with them,
and how he had opened a door of faith for the Gentiles. Acts 14:27

Paul and Barnabas Confirm the Gentile Mission

ACTS 14:21-28 *²¹After they had proclaimed the good news to that city and had made many disciples, they returned to Lystra, then on to Iconium and Antioch. ²²There they strengthened the souls of the disciples and encouraged them to continue in the faith, saying, "It is through many persecutions that we must enter the kingdom of God." ²³And after they had appointed elders for them in each church, with prayer and fasting they entrusted them to the Lord in whom they had come to believe.*

²⁴Then they passed through Pisidia and came to Pamphylia. ²⁵When they had spoken the word in Perga, they went down to Attalia. ²⁶From there they sailed back to Antioch, where they had been commended to the grace of God for the work that they had completed. ²⁷When they arrived, they called the church together and related all that God had done with them, and how he had opened a door of faith for the Gentiles. ²⁸And they stayed there with the disciples for some time.

The billions of Christians who form the worldwide church today descend from a few thousand scattered throughout the Roman empire of the first century. The thousands of dioceses that constitute the church today are the heirs of the few dozen local churches founded or visited by apostles and missionaries in the ancient Mediterranean world. Thanks to the committed zeal of people like Paul and Barnabas and their coworkers, these early communities received a firm foundation and expanded to become the global church of our day.

Acts offers us a breathless recital of the journeys of these evangelizers from city to city as they establish new churches and exhort existing churches, encouraging them to persevere in the faith despite many hardships. In their planting and nurturing of new communities, these missionaries were convinced that God's grace was guiding and empowering them. Their own suffering for the faith and perseverance in the mission were inspiring examples for the communities and gave credibility to their leadership.

From Derbe, Paul and Barnabas return to Lystra, Iconium, and Pisidian Antioch. In each place, they encourage these young communities to continue in the faith and warn them that trials and persecutions are sure to come. Discerning the need to stabilize the young churches with local leadership, they wisely appoint "elders," or presbyters, in each community, but only after prayer and fasting (verse 23). They entrust them to the Lord, confident that they will carry on the work after the apostles have departed. They also return through the regions of Pisidia and Pamphylia, including Perga and Attalia, before they sail back to Antioch in Syria, the church that had commissioned them for their missionary work (verse 26).

On arriving in Antioch, the first mission is complete. Paul and Barnabas report "all that God had done with them" (Acts 14:27). They know they are not individual adventurists, but apostles. They have been sent out, commissioned as God's instruments to communicate the good news of Jesus Christ far and wide. And they gladly report that God has "opened the door of faith to the Gentiles" (14:27) through their mission.

This "door of faith" that God opened through the ministry of Paul and Barnabas is always open now for all people. When the word of God is proclaimed and the heart allows itself to be shaped by transforming grace, anyone is able to cross the threshold of that "door of faith" and enter into the life of discipleship. Through turning to God in repentance and belief and through the gift of the Holy Spirit, all people are able to enter Christ's church and begin the lifelong journey of salvation through sharing in communion with God.

Reflection and discussion

• What characteristics of the apostles' ministry among the churches is most inspiring to you? What lessons can our church today learn from Paul and Barnabas and their coworkers?

• Jesus does not envision his church as a closed circle of mutually exchanged love, but one that keeps widening outward. What can I do this week to love expansively and to be a missionary to others?

• Why is the image of the "door of faith" a good metaphor describing the Christian life? What does one encounter when stepping across the threshold?

Prayer

Lord God, you have done great things for us through the gift of your Holy Spirit working within us and among us. Thank you for opening the door of faith to me and leading me into the life of Jesus your Son. Give me the grace to continue receiving your word of life and to invite others across the threshold into your kingdom.

SUGGESTIONS FOR FACILITATORS, GROUP SESSION 6

1. Welcome group members and make any final announcements or requests.

2. You may want to pray this prayer as a group:

God of all peoples, your apostles experienced trials, persecution, imprisonment, and martyrdom in their witness to the gospel. May the lives of Peter and John and of Paul and Barnabas inspire us to reach out beyond our comforts to a world in need of your saving word. Help us to experience your call and to discern the unique mission you have chosen for each one of us. As we study your inspired word, teach us how Jesus is the key to unlock the treasures of Scripture, and show us how to be evangelizers. May we know those things that we ought to do and those things that we must patiently leave in your hands.

3. Ask one or more of the following questions:
   - How has this study of the Acts of the Apostles enriched your life?
   - In what way has this study challenged you the most?

4. Discuss lessons 25 through 30. Choose one or more of the questions for reflection and discussion from each lesson to discuss as a group.

5. Ask the group if they would like to study another in the Threshold Bible Study series. Discuss the topic and dates, and make a decision among those interested. Ask the group members to suggest people they would like to invite to participate in the next study series.

6. Ask the group to discuss the insights that stand out most from this study over the past six weeks.

7. Conclude by praying aloud the following prayer or another of your own choosing:

Holy Spirit of the living God, you inspired the writers of the Scriptures and you have guided our study during these weeks. Continue to deepen our love for the word of God in the holy Scriptures, and draw us more deeply into the heart of Jesus. We thank you for the confident hope you have placed within us and the gifts that build up the church. Through this study, lead us to worship and witness more fully and fervently, and bless us now and always with the fire of your love.

The
ACTS OF THE
APOSTLES
in the Sunday Lectionary

READING
Sunday or feast
(Lectionary #-Cycle)

ACTS 1:1-11
Ascension of the Lord
(58-ABC)

ACTS 1:12-14
7th Sunday of Easter
(59-A)

ACTS 1:15-17, 20A, 20C-26
7th Sunday of Easter
(60-B)

ACTS 2:1-11
Pentecost Sunday
(63-ABC)

ACTS 2:14, 22-33
3rd Sunday of Easter
(46-A)

ACTS 2:14A, 36-41
4th Sunday of Easter
(49-A)

ACTS 2:42-47
2nd Sunday of Easter
(43-A)

ACTS 3:13-15, 17-19
3rd Sunday of Easter
(47-B)

THE ACTS OF THE APOSTLES IN THE SUNDAY LECTIONARY

ACTS 4:8-12
4th Sunday of Easter
(50-B)

ACTS 4:32-35
2nd Sunday of Easter
(44-B)

ACTS 5:12-16
2nd Sunday of Easter
(45-C)

ACTS 5:27-32, 40B-41
3rd Sunday of Easter
(48-C)

ACTS 6:1-7
5th Sunday of Easter
(52-A)

ACTS 7:55-60
7th Sunday of Easter
(61-C)

ACTS 8:5-8, 14-17
6th Sunday of Easter
(55-A)

ACTS 9:26-31
5th Sunday of Easter
(53-B)

ACTS 10:25-26, 34-35, 44-48
6th Sunday of Easter
(56-B)

ACTS 10:34-38
Sunday after Epiphany: Baptism of the Lord
(21-ABC)

ACTS 10:34A, 37-43
Easter Sunday: Resurrection of the Lord
(42-ABC)

ACTS 13:14, 43-52
4th Sunday of Easter
(51-C)

ACTS 13:16-17, 22-25
Christmas: Vigil Mass
(13-ABC)

ACTS 14:21-27
5th Sunday of Easter
(54-C)

ACTS 15:1-2, 22-29
6th Sunday of Easter
(57-C)

Ordering Additional Studies

AVAILABLE TITLES IN THIS SERIES INCLUDE...

Advent Light

Angels of God

Divine Mercy

Eucharist

The Feasts of Judaism

God's Spousal Love

The Holy Spirit and Spiritual Gifts

Jerusalem, the Holy City

Missionary Discipleship

Mysteries of the Rosary

The Names of Jesus

Peacemaking and Nonviolence

People of the Passion

Pilgrimage in the Footsteps of Jesus

The Resurrection and the Life

The Sacred Heart of Jesus

Stewardship of the Earth

The Tragic and Triumphant Cross

Church of the Holy Spirit
(Part 1): Acts of the Apostles 1–14

Church of the Holy Spirit
(Part 2): Acts of the Apostles 15–28

Jesus, the Word Made Flesh
(Part 1): John 1–10

Jesus, the Word Made Flesh
(Part 2): John 11–21

Jesus, the Compassionate Savior
(Part 1): Luke 1–11

Jesus, the Compassionate Savior
(Part 2): Luke 12–24

Jesus, the Suffering Servant
(Part 1): Mark 1–8

Jesus, the Suffering Servant
(Part 2): Mark 9–16

Jesus, the Messianic King
(Part 1): Matthew 1–16

Jesus, the Messianic King
(Part 2): Matthew 17–28

The Lamb and the Beasts:
The Book of Revelation

Salvation Offered for All People: Romans

TWENTY-THIRD PUBLICATIONS

TO CHECK AVAILABILITY OR FOR A DESCRIPTION
OF EACH STUDY, VISIT OUR WEBSITE AT
www.ThresholdBibleStudy.com
OR CALL US AT **1-800-321-0411**